U.S. History Activities

Interactive Learning Strategies and Enrichment Projects

John Zola

Ron Schukar

About the authors

John Zola taught high school and middle school history and social studies for 32 years in Wisconsin and Colorado. He also taught social studies methods courses at the University of Colorado-Boulder; as well as conducting a broad range of professional development workshops and authoring curriculum on a variety of social studies topics.

Ron Schukar taught high school social studies before serving as the Director for the Center for Teaching International Relations in the Graduate School of International Studies at the University of Denver. He has also conducted numerous teacher training workshops and written curriculum on global studies and other social studies topics.

Acknowledgements

John Zola would like to thank the students who have been willing to experiment with different ways of learning and the following individuals who have contributed their ideas and insights to the development of activities included in this volume: Ranne Dwyer, Reny Sieck, Jackie Johnson, Doug Superka, Bruce Tipple, Tom Tonnesen, and most importantly, Jaye Zola.

Ron Schukar would like to thank his family, colleagues, and friends for their ideas, constructive criticism, patience, and support

This book was previously published as *Getting Involved: Enrichment Projects and Activities for United States History* by: Pearson Education, Inc.

Contents

Using Getting Involved

The purpose of *Getting Involved* activities is to enrich and enliven United States history by providing active learning strategies that engage students in understanding key concepts, events, and issues. All 32 activities are designed to bring both rigor and action into the classroom by helping students expand their learning beyond their textbooks.

The major teaching strategies used in *Getting Involved* are described below. Tips on evaluating student participation and learning in each strategy are also provided.

Small/Large Group Discussion

The small/large group discussion strategy differs from common classroom discussion in following a prescribed sequence. First, the teacher introduces the topic through a short, motivational presentation of basic information. This establishes a supportive climate and a positive attitude toward participation. Next, students are divided into small groups to examine relevant information, discuss alternative approaches, and reach a conclusion. In the final step the entire class participates in a summary discussion to synthesize information and promote critical thinking. One example of this strategy is Activity 2, which uses small/large group discussion to expand understanding of the goals and motivations of European explorers.

Evaluation Tips: Focus on both the amount and quality of participation by recording points students earn in the course of discussions. Note frequency with which students initiate dialogue, respond actively, listen, clarify, and question. Criteria for assessing quality of ideas may include clarity, organization, and logic.

Cooperative Learning

In the cooperative learning strategy, students work in small groups. However, unlike other small group work, in cooperative learning groups each student has a clearly defined task that is integral to the success of the whole group. Activity 17, in which students interpret the 1912 Progressive party platform, is one example of how individual accountability is built into cooperative group projects. Cooperative learning has a variety of formats, including "jigsaw learning." In the jigsaw format, each student in a small group becomes an expert on one part of the assigned material. After developing expertise, students teach each other what they learn.

Evaluation Tips: Because cooperative learning makes students dependent on each other, it is usually not necessary to grade their participation in small group work. It is important, however, to assess content learning. One way is to test groups rather than individuals, giving every member of a group the same grade. Another technique is to test students individually, average the scores of all students within a group, and give each student in the group the average score.

Debates: Historical and Contemporary

Debates help students identify different viewpoints on a topic or issue and learn to support viewpoints with specific arguments and evidence. In historical debates, students gather information from primary and secondary sources. In contemporary debates, current media information may be added to older primary and secondary sources. It is not necessary to follow the rules of formal debate, but the general format of having students state specific positions, provide evidence and supporting arguments, and rebut opposing arguments should be followed.

Debates differ from discussion in that sides are chosen and defended or opposed without seeking compromise or resolution. You may use peer evaluation of debates by having a panel of students judge the debates and select the more convincing side. Classroom debates are most effective when followed with a discussion in which the best arguments are identified and individual conclusions drawn. Activity 23 uses historical debate to help students decide what foreign policy to follow regarding a fictitious Central American nation in the 1920s.

Evaluation Tips: To ensure good preparation, you may evaluate students' preparation notes. One technique for assessing participation in the debate itself is to score each student's presentation on a scale of 1 to 5. Highest scores go to the presentations demonstrating the best use of factual data and logic. Explain the scoring system before the debate. To ensure polite and attentive behavior through the debate, you may take away points for rude behavior.

Dilemmas: Historical and Contemporary

The dilemma strategy is based on a written case study which poses a difficult choice. For example, Activity 10 describes the events leading up to the Mexican-American War and requires students to decide whether Congress should declare war on Mexico. Reasons for and against making particular choices are embedded in the dilemma. Students must identify and develop rationales for the choice they make. There are no right or wrong answers in dilemmas, but students must support their choices. Students' individual reading and consideration of dilemmas should culminate in a class discussion or debate that exposes them to the reasoning of others.

Evaluation Tips: Participation in a class discussion or debate on a dilemma may be scored on the point system suggested for evaluating classroom debates. In addition, you may direct students to prepare a "pros and cons" sheet on which they identify their solution to the dilemma, then list and describe the pros and cons of that choice. For a more detailed assessment, you may require students to write an essay in which they take and defend a position on the dilemma.

Role Play

Role play is a group problem-solving technique in which individual students assume the identity of another person. Role playing encourages students to examine and evaluate an event or concept from a personal perspective that may be quite different from their own. Role plays may vary in length from short scenes to more extended situations and may focus on historical or contemporary situations. One example of this strategy is Activity 15, in which students role play people in the late 1800s who are for or against technological development. Role plays provide students with a safe environment for exploring and understanding viewpoints held by other people.

Evaluation Tips: You may base evaluation on individual and group preparation, authenticity of information used to develop the roles, willingness to represent views different from one's own, ability to suspend judgment during the role play, and enthusiasm for participating. Although students should not be evaluated on their dramatic abilities, you may recognize outstanding performances.

Simulation

Simulation is a technique designed to immerse participants in situations or events that replicate "real life" as closely as possible. In simulations, not only do students assume the identities of other people, but they also act out their roles according to the rules, systems, structures, and other variables inherent in actual situations. Simulations differ from role plays in that they incorporate more detail and generally take longer than role plays. Often simulations involve problem solving or decision making. For example, in Activity 11 students simulate the differences between craft and mass production methods. Simulation, and a follow-up debriefing, will help students understand events or problems that lie beyond their personal experience.

Evaluation Tips: You may evaluate student participation on preparation for the role play, attention in following the simulation rules, seriousness of effort, and appropriate use of conflict resolution skills. In the debriefing, evaluate students on their ability to make connections between the simulation and actual situations or events.

Data Collection and Oral History Interviews

As a teaching strategy, data collection refers to collecting, analyzing, and manipulating statistical or other empirical data for the purpose of explaining phenomena, drawing general conclusions, or forecasting. The data may be historical or contemporary. Activity 31, in which students collect data from newspapers to forecast future trends, is one example.

The oral history interview is a form of data collection. In this strategy, students use personal interviews to collect information. They record interviewees' responses in writing or on tape. Oral history interviews help students gather information and draw conclusions based on others' firsthand experiences. For example, in Activity 21 students interview survivors of the Great Depression to gather information on its impact. Oral history interviews are most effective when students summarize and reflect on the interviews by contributing to a class discussion or writing a report.

Evaluation Tips: You may evaluate students on the number and reliability of sources they use, their visual or verbal presentations of data, and the reasonableness of the generalizations or conclusions they draw. Share evaluation criteria with students before they begin their collection activities.

Evaluation of student work in an oral history interview activity may include assessment of both a process and a final product. Criteria for assessing the interview process may include proof of adequate planning (in the form of a written copy of questions) and evidence of appropriate interview interaction (in the form of interview notes). Written reports and contributions to class discussions may be evaluated on clarity of information and logic of conclusions drawn from the data collected.

Individual and Paired Writing

In both individual and paired writing strategies, the primary task for students is to create a final written product. Individual writing projects may take the form of letters, editorials, articles, essays, poetry, stories, and journal entries. Paired writing is a "deliberate discussion" in written form. In pairs, students discuss an assigned topic through a written dialogue in which one student states a position and the other student responds, then states another position. For example, in Activity 9 students engage in a paired writing task in which one supports and the other opposes the institution of slavery. The expected final product is a written dialogue of several pages in length.

Evaluation Tips: Evaluate individual writing projects on adherence to the style of writing assigned (article, letter, etc.), accuracy and clarity of the content, and appropriate use of language. Evaluate paired writing tasks on participation and final products. During their writing time the students should either be writing or quietly preparing their ideas. Written dialogues should reflect focus on the topic and thoughtful response to each other. You may give students individual or pair grades on their dialogues.

Art Projects

Art projects provide students with an opportunity to express their understanding of social studies content in visual formats. They provide a change of pace for students and offer success to those for whom written and oral expression is difficult. You may assign art projects as either individual or small group tasks. Activity 12, in which students create posters illustrating interpretations of the causes of the Civil War, is one example of an art project.

Evaluation Tips: To ensure that students seriously attend to an art project, state the criteria for evaluation when giving the assignment. Projects should not be evaluated on artistic talent but rather on accuracy in reflecting the project's content and the care with which the project is completed. In the case of group work, part of each member's grade should be for staying on task and cooperating with the group.

About the Activity

In this activity students try their hand at being historians. Examining bank checks, they draw their own conclusions about the lives of a father and son. By exploring this "mystery," they see more clearly that history is both fact and interpretation.

After participating in the activity, students will be able to

- define the term *history*.
- analyze historical evidence for patterns and relationships.
- write an historical account from evidence.
- recognize that history includes subjective interpretation of facts.

Planning for the Activity

Suggested Time: 2 class periods

Materials: Activity Sheets 1a and 1b, one each per student

Advance Preparation: Familiarize yourself with the evidence on the sheets, forming hypotheses about the actions and motives of the people involved.

THE ACTIVITY

Getting Started

Introduce this activity by asking students to write down their own definitions of *history*. Have volunteers share their definitions, and note the common characteristics among them. Then discuss the following statements:

- History is a record or account, usually written and in chronological order, of past events. (Funk and Wagnalls Standard Dictionary)
- History extends and elaborates memory by interpreting relics and synthesizing reports from past eyewitnesses; historians study the past by scrutinizing accounts of what has happened in the real world. (Historian David Lowenthal)

Continue the discussion by asking students the following questions:

- What is meant by historical evidence? Does evidence consist only of facts? What is the difference between facts and opinions? What roles do facts and opinions play in history?
- Can the work of historians ever be objective? Ask students to suggest personal and historical examples in which a person's values might affect his or her account of an event.

COMMENTS/NOTES

One personal example of how values affect interpretation is the difference in the way a teen and a parent might describe a curfew violation. An historical example is the difference in British and American historians' interpretations of Revolutionary War causes.

Teaching

Explain that although historians agree on many details of history, there are still disputes over how to interpret historical evidence to determine the causes, effects, and significance of events. Then tell the class they will now have a chance to become historians themselves.

1. Distribute Activity Sheets 1a and 1b. They constitute the evidence: a series of checks written between 1903 and 1931.

2. Divide the class into groups of three to five students. Have them try to construct the historical circumstances in which the checks were written. Suggest that they look for patterns and relationships in the information.

3. After 20 minutes, have volunteers present their interpretations. Ask them to analyze how values may have affected their views.

4. For homework, assign students to write their own narratives of the events suggested by the checks. Emphasize that their accounts must be logical, supported by evidence, and written in a two- to three-page narrative format. They should not simply summarize the information on the checks.

Concluding

On the due date, ask volunteers to read their accounts aloud. Have the class compare these interpretations. Ask students to discuss how they decided which information to include and exclude. Have them analyze how much of their accounts can be factually documented and how much is interpretation. Encourage them to identify how their own values affected their interpretations. Conclude with a discussion of why history is never just facts.

Evaluating Student Work

Criteria for evaluating papers should include:

- narrative presentation rather than a listing.
- logic in drawing conclusions.
- acceptable writing quality.

Background. Historian David Lowenthal writes that no historical account ever corresponds precisely with the actual past because history is limited by the immensity of the past, the distinction between actual events and accounts of them, and bias in interpretation.

Background. The "evidence" on the activity sheets first appeared in a 1932 *Vanity Fair* article titled "Ordeal by Checque," which left the task of interpretation up to the readers.

Point out to students that in writing their narratives, they will need to emphasize some data and ignore other data as they decide what is important to recreating the Exeters' story.

History: Not Just Facts
Interpreting Evidence to Write History

Date	Payable to	Amount	Signed
8/30/03	Goosie Gander Baby Shoppe	$148.00	Lawrence Exeter
9/2/03	Hollywood Hospital	$100.00	Lawrence Exeter
10/3/03	Dr. David M. McCoy	$475.00	Lawrence Exeter, Sr.
12/19/03	California Toyland Co.	$83.20	Lawrence Exeter, Sr.
10/6/09	Palisades School for Boys	$1,250.00	Lawrence Exeter, Sr.
4/18/10	City Bicycle Co.	$52.50	Lawrence Exeter, Sr.
8/26/15	Columbia Military Academy	$2,150.00	Lawrence Exeter, Sr.
9/3/21	Hollywood Cadillac Co.	$3,885.00	Lawrence Exeter, Sr.
9/7/21	Wilshire Auto Repair	$288.76	Lawrence Exeter, Sr.
10/15/21	Stanford University	$339.00	Lawrence Exeter, Sr.
6/1/23	Miss Daisy Windsor	$25,000.00	Lawrence Exeter, Sr.
6/9/23	French Line	$585.00	Lawrence Exeter, Sr.
8/23/23	Banque de France	$5,000.00	Lawrence Exeter, Sr.
2/13/26	University Club Florists	$76.50	Lawrence Exeter, Sr.
6/23/26	University Club Florists	$312.75	Lawrence Exeter, Sr.
8/11/26	Riviera Heights Land Co.	$56,000.00	Lawrence Exeter, Sr.
10/30/26	Renaissance Interior Decorators	$22,000.00	Lawrence Exeter, Sr.
11/16/26	Hawaii Steamship Co.	$560.00	Lawrence Exeter, Sr.
11/18/26	Beverly Diamond and Gift Shop	$678.00	Lawrence Exeter, Sr.
11/21/26	Lawrence Exeter, Junior	$200,000.00	Lawrence Exeter, Sr.
11/22/26	Ambassador Hotel	$2,250.00	Lawrence Exeter, Sr.
12/1/26	University Club Florists	$183.50	Lawrence Exeter, Sr.

History: Not Just Facts
Interpreting Evidence to Write History

Date	Payable to	Amount	Signed
2/18/26	Coconut Grove Sweet Shoppe	$27.00	Lawrence Exeter, Jr.
7/16/27	Parisian Gown Shoppe	$925.00	Lawrence Exeter, Jr.
12/1/27	Anita Lingerie Salon	$750.00	Lawrence Exeter, Jr.
4/1/28	Parisian Gown Shoppe	$1,150.00	Lawrence Exeter, Jr.
11/1/28	Moderne Sportte Shoppe	$562.00	Lawrence Exeter, Jr.
7/1/29	The Bootery	$145.25	Lawrence Exeter, Jr.
8/23/29	Tony Spagoni	$126.00	Lawrence Exeter, Jr.
8/30/29	Tony Spagoni	$126.00	Lawrence Exeter, Jr.
5/25/30	University Club Florists	$87.00	Lawrence Exeter, Jr.
5/28/30	Broadway Diamond Co.	$575.00	Lawrence Exeter, Jr.
11/13/30	Miss Flossie Wentworth	$50,000.00	Lawrence Exeter, Jr.
11/14/30	Wall & Smith, Attorneys at Law	$525.00	Lawrence Exeter, Jr.
11/15/30	Mrs. Lawrence Exeter, Jr.	$5,000.00	Lawrence Exeter, Jr.
6/20/31	Clerk, Reno Municipal Court	$52.00	Lawrence Exeter, Jr.
6/20/31	Marie Wharton Exeter	$175,000.00	Lawrence Exeter, Jr.
6/20/31	Walker & Walker	$700.00	Lawrence Exeter, Jr.
6/20/31	Wall & Smith	$450.00	Lawrence Exeter, Jr.
7/1/31	Tony Spagoni	$100.00	Lawrence Exeter, Jr.
7/2/31	Tony Spagoni	$100.00	Lawrence Exeter, Jr.
7/3/31	Peter Ventizzi	$25.00	Lawrence Exeter, Jr.
7/5/31	Hollywood Hospital	$100.00	Lawrence Exeter, Sr.
7/15/31	Dr. David M. McCoy	$175.00	Lawrence Exeter
7/16/31	Hollywood Mortuary	$1,280.00	Lawrence Exeter

I'll Go to the Ends of the Earth for You
Deciding Among Exploration Proposals

About the Activity

What were the risks and possible benefits of the European voyages of exploration during the 1400s and 1500s? In this activity, students play the roles of European rulers trying to decide whether to support various expedition proposals. The activity is most effective when used *before* studying the voyages, for it helps to make the human drama of the "age of exploration" more real to students.

After participating in the activity, students will be able to

- describe the exploration goals of John Cabot, Ponce de León, Hernando Cortés, Jacques Cartier, and Francis Drake.
- write an essay describing the value and effects of each explorer's voyage.
- compare the explorations of early Europeans with present-day explorations.

Planning for the Activity

Suggested Time: 1 class period

Materials: Activity Sheet 2

THE ACTIVITY

Getting Started

Ask students to name early European explorers they remember from previous history classes. Post the names on the chalkboard and have students describe what they remember about the goals and effects of the expeditions.

Teaching

Ask students to imagine that they are rulers of a European nation such as England, France, Spain, or Portugal in the late 1400s or the 1500s. Explain that as rulers they are often approached by adventurers who have grand ideas for exploring distant lands. Each promises that his explorations will bring the nation riches, power, and glory.

1. Distribute Activity Sheet 2 to each student. Review the directions and allow about five minutes for each student to rank the top three proposals.

2. Organize students into groups of three to five. Direct members of each group to compare their individual rankings and then to agree on which three proposals to fund. In their deliberations, students should try to convince others of their views while remaining open to opposing arguments. Allow about 10 to 15 minutes for this group discussion.

COMMENTS/NOTES

Background. Remind students that the question of whether the world was flat or round had been settled well before the days of Columbus and his fellow European explorers. However, these early sailors greatly underestimated the size of the earth; the errors contributed to their belief that the Americas were the Far East.

3. Reconvene the class and compare group rankings. Discuss the relative merits and potential benefits of each proposal.

4. Explain that each proposal briefly describes goals of an actual European adventurer who explored areas of the Western Hemisphere in the late 1400s or the 1500s. Challenge them, as individuals, to identify the explorer whose goals are described in each proposal. (1 Francis Drake, 2 John Cabot, 3 Hernando Cortés, 4 Jacques Cartier, 5 Juan Ponce de León.)

5. Explain that as they study the age of exploration, they will learn about the outcomes of each explorer's expedition. Direct them to write an essay describing the value of each exploration to the sponsoring nation and the effects of the explorations on the peoples of the Americas and other European nations.

Concluding

Lead a class discussion on the dilemmas faced by the rulers who had to decide which explorers to support. Ask students to speculate about voyages that may have been proposed but never funded. Where might the explorers have proposed going? What benefits might they have promised the rulers?

Encourage students to compare early European explorations with present-day space and ocean explorations. Discuss issues involved in funding such projects as building a space station, sending humans to Mars, and exploring ocean depths. Compare the benefits claimed by early explorers with those claimed by today's advocates of exploration. Then compare the potential negative impact of future exploration with the negative outcomes of early European exploration.

Evaluating Student Work

Small group work may be informally evaluated by monitoring the groups and assessing each student's contributions and attentive listening.

Criteria for evaluating essays should include accuracy of factual information, logic in describing cause-and-effect relationships, and clarity in identifying costs and benefits of expeditions.

Encourage, or require, students to research each of the explorers in resource books as well as in their texts. Direct them to focus on the outcomes of the expeditions.

Background. As an example of the impact of one expedition on the peoples of the Americas, point out that one of Cortés's allies in defeating the Aztecs was the smallpox with which his men inadvertently infected the Indians, who had no immunity to this previously unknown disease.

I'll Go to the Ends of the Earth for You
Deciding Among Exploration Proposals

Directions

You are a ruler of a powerful European nation during the age of exploration. Many adventurers come to you, seeking financial support for voyages of exploration and conquest. Each comes with a plan designed to convince you that he can gain fantastic wealth and new territory for your nation. Unfortunately, you cannot afford to fund every proposal. Read the following proposals and choose the three you will support. Be prepared to state reasons for your choices.

PROPOSAL 1   I propose sailing to the New World to seek a northern sea route to Japan and the riches of the Orient. Provide me with money and support, and I will find a new route that will bring wealth and power to your nation. I will need only a small crew of eighteen men and will give you one fifth of the treasures I find.

PROPOSAL 2   It is rumored that wealth beyond imagination lies in the unexplored world across the sea. My men and I seek your support to sail to these lands and return with gold and silver to fill your treasury. As we explore, we will claim the lands in your name and convert the natives from their heathen religions to Christianity. With control of these new lands and peoples, your nation will become the most powerful on earth.

PROPOSAL 3   I know I can bring wealth in the form of gold and precious metals from the lands across the sea. However, we must also explore and chart this unknown land. I seek your support to journey to the northern areas of the "New World," to chart the waterways and begin settlements. These settlements will assure your claim to the new lands and their riches.

PROPOSAL 4   What is wealth to a king who must at some point die? I propose to search for the fabled Fountain of Youth and to return with its magic waters. This is certainly worth more than any amount of gold and silver. However, my men and I will also fill your treasury as we conquer the new lands and claim them for you.

PROPOSAL 5   Provide me with necessary funds, and I will bring fame and fortune to our great nation. I will raid the ships of our enemies, seize their cargoes, sink their vessels, and bring back wealth untold. My raids will challenge and defeat our enemies so that we can become the greatest nation on earth. I realize you may have to deny knowledge of me and my activities to make it appear that you do not approve of them.

About the Activity

Imagining themselves to be foreign travelers through England's American colonies in 1730, students write journals describing conditions in the three colonial regions.

After participating in the activity, students will be able to

- assess the value of using primary sources, such as journals, in studying history.
- describe the similarities and differences in colonial life in the New England, Middle, and Southern colonies in the mid-1700s.
- identify problems regional differences may have created in colonial America.

Planning for the Activity

Suggested Time: 2 class periods.

Materials: Activity Sheets 3a and 3b, one each per student

THE ACTIVITY

Getting Started

Introduce the activity by asking students to discuss this question: If you were to live in another country for one or two years, what information about the country would you be interested in learning? Record students' responses on the chalkboard.

Next, ask the class to discuss what they think visitors from other countries would want to learn about life and people in the United States. Have students consider how visitors' impressions might be influenced by the places they chose to visit. For example, would travelers' impressions be different if they visited a small town rather than a large city, or a state in the Southwest rather than one in the Northeast?

Teaching

Explain to students that they are asked to imagine themselves to be foreign visitors to the American colonies in the mid-1700s. They will write journals describing daily life in the New England, Middle, or Southern colonial region.

1. On the chalkboard, write *New England Colonies, Middle Colonies,* and *Southern Colonies.* Have students name the specific colonies in each region. (New England: Massachusetts, New Hampshire, Rhode Island, Connecticut; Middle Colonies: Pennsylvania, Delaware, New York, New Jersey; Southern Colonies: Virginia, Maryland, North Carolina, South Carolina, Georgia.)

COMMENTS/NOTES

If you have a foreign-exchange student or a recent arrival in your class, ask him or her to share impressions of your community.

2. Explain that visitors sometimes recorded their observations in journals. Then distribute copies of Activity Sheet 3a, which contains excerpts from a journal written by Andrew Burnaby, an English minister who traveled through the American colonies in 1759 and 1760. After students read the excerpts, discuss with them the following questions:

- In what aspects of colonial life and society was Burnaby most interested?

- According to Burnaby, how did colonists in New York differ from those in Virginia?

- What was Burnaby's view of slavery?

3. Distribute copies of Activity Sheet 3b and review the instructions. Divide the class so that one third are assigned to each region. Allow time for students, as individuals, to complete their research and write their entries.

Concluding

After students have completed their journals, divide the class into groups of three to five, with each group having representatives from each of the three colonial regions. Allow 15 minutes for students to share some of their observations and to draw conclusions about similarities and differences among the colonial regions.

Conclude the activity with a class discussion of the following questions:

- In what ways was life in the colonial regions similar? In what ways was life different? What factors account for the differences?

- What problems, if any, may have resulted from regional differences?

- Is there any evidence that regional differences still exist today? Explain.

Evaluating Student Work

Options for evaluating student work in this activity include the following:

- assessing students' participation in group discussion by observing their contributions, their willingness to listen to each other, and their thoughtfulness in drawing conclusions.

- assessing journals using criteria such as accuracy, thoroughness, creativity, and appropriate use of language.

Point out that although the observations of some foreign travelers were accurate and insightful, others gave biased or inaccurate accounts of life in the Americas.

Background. Andrew Burnaby was born in 1734. In 1759 and 1760, he traveled through the American colonies. A Christian minister and a loyal supporter of the English crown, he recorded his impressions in a journal that was published in 1775.

_____

_____

_____

Encourage students to use their texts and other reference materials as sources of information. Journal writing may be assigned as homework.

_____

_____

_____

_____

_____

_____

_____

_____

_____

_____

_____

_____

_____

_____

Reflections on a Colonial Journey
Excerpts from an English Traveler's Journal

The following excerpts are from *Travels Through the Middle Settlements in North America in the Years 1759 and 1760 with Observations Upon the State of the Colonies*. The journal's author was Andrew Burnaby, an English minister.

Virginia

From what has been said of the colony, it will not be difficult to form an idea of the character of its inhabitants. The climate and external appearance of the country conspire to make them indolent, easy, and good natured; extremely fond of society and much given to convivial pleasures. In consequence of this, they seldom show any spirit of enterprise, or expose themselves willingly to fatigue. Their authority over their slaves renders them vain and imperious, and entire strangers to that elegance of sentiment which is so peculiarly characteristic of refined and polished nations. Their ignorance of mankind and learning exposes them to many errors and prejudices, especially in regard to Indians and Negroes, whom they scarcely consider as of the human species.

New York

The inhabitants of New York, in their character, very much resemble the Pennsylvanians: more than half of them are Dutch, and almost all traders: they are, therefore, habitually frugal, industrious, and parsimonious. Being, however, of different nations, different languages, and different religions, it is almost impossible to give them any precise or determinate character.

Massachusetts Bay

The government of this province is lodged in the hands of a governor or lieutenant governor, appointed by the king; a council of twenty-eight persons, chosen annually, with the governor's approbation, by the general assembly; and a house of representatives annually elected by the freeholders.

New Hampshire

The chief articles of exportation are fish, cattle, ships, of which they annually build near 200, and masts for the royal navy. These are made of white pine, and are, I believe, the finest in the world, many of them being forty yards long, and as many inches in diameter. They never cut them down but in times of deep snow, as it would be impossible in any other season to get them down to the river. Then the trees are fallen, they yoke seventy or eighty pair of oxen, and drag them along the snow.

Pennsylvania

As to religion, there is none properly established; but Protestants of all denominations, Papists, Jews, and all other sects whatsoever, are universally tolerated. There are twelve clergymen of the Church of England, who are sent by the Society for the Propagation of the Gospel.

Reflections on a Colonial Journey
Writing a Traveler's Journal

Background

You are a traveler from England who has come to North America in 1730. You will be observing life and society in the New England, Middle, or Southern colonies and reporting your findings.

Directions

Make a three-day record of your travel observations and thoughts in a journal. Among the topics you might include are geography, natural resources, social classes, jobs, religion, housing, food and drink, social customs, agriculture, politics, education, industry, trade, relationships with Native Americans, transportation, indentured servants, and slavery.

Use your text and other reference materials as sources of information. Give your journal a name on the title line below, and then start your entries. The dates for your entries should be June 8, 9, and 10, 1730. Continue your journal on additional sheets of paper.

_____

June 8, 1730

_____

_____

_____

_____

_____

_____

_____

_____

_____

_____

_____

_____

_____

_____

On the Road to Revolution
Reenacting Pre-Revolutionary War Events

 *Activity* **4**

About the Activity

Becoming minidrama playwrights and actors, students work in small groups to dramatize major events that led up to the Revolutionary War. This activity should be conducted after students have studied the period of 1763 to 1776.

After participating in the activity, students will be able to

- create a minidrama identifying key aspects of key pre-Revolutionary War events.
- recognize relationships between pre-Revolutionary War events and aspects of our present-day government, economy, and national values.

Planning for the Activity

Suggested Time: 2 class periods

Advance Preparation: Prepare six slips of paper with the following labels: Proclamation of 1763, Sugar Act, Quartering Act, Stamp Act, Townshend Acts, Intolerable Acts.

THE ACTIVITY

Getting Started

Begin by asking the class to name events during the period 1763–1776 that are considered causes of the Revolutionary War. Post students' responses on the chalkboard. Challenge them to number the events in chronological order.

Teaching

Tell the class that they will be exploring issues and events that led to the Revolutionary War by preparing and presenting minidramas.

1. Divide the class into groups of three to four. Have each group randomly draw one of the six slips of paper. If there are more than six groups, collect the topic slips after the sixth choice and continue drawing.

2. Explain that each group is to prepare a minidrama for the topic they drew. The dramas will be performed for the class. Specify these guidelines:

- Every group member must have an active role.
- The topic must be presented both clearly and accurately.
- The drama may involve humor, but the task must be taken seriously.

COMMENTS/NOTES

You may wish to encourage groups to reenact more than one topic, perhaps for extra credit.

■ The drama must present opposing viewpoints on the topic.

A drama might present an argument between colonists affected by a law and British officials enforcing it. For example, a minidrama on the Quartering Act might open with a married couple discussing their hope that no British soldiers will intrude on their home. When a British soldier knocks at their door, the ensuing dialogue brings out the fact that the couple was forced by law to give him shelter. The drama might reflect a mutual contempt between the colonists and the soldier.

Allow groups at least 30-45 minutes to create and rehearse their minidramas. Encourage them to use their texts and other resources.

3. Have the groups present their dramas in chronological order, beginning with the Proclamation of 1763.

Concluding

When all the minidramas have been presented, discuss the following questions.

■ How did the cumulative effect of the laws and proclamations persuade colonists to seek independence from Britain?

■ Of the events dramatized, which do you think were of greater and lesser importance in increasing support for independence? Why?

■ What aspects of our present-day legislative process, judicial system, economy, and society may have developed in response to various British acts during the colonial period?

Evaluating Student Work

See "Additional Background Information" for key understandings related to each topic. This activity is appropriate for peer evaluation. Before each presentation, appoint members of two other groups to evaluate the upcoming minidrama, using the guidelines noted in Step 2 of the "Teaching" section. Have each evaluator succinctly state the presentation's strengths and weaknesses. Share relevant student evaluations with the performers.

Background. The Quartering Act seems particularly unusual to us today. The law was enacted to make the colonists pay part of Britain's costs of keeping troops in America. By the act's terms, colonists were required to supply soldiers with living quarters, fuel, candles, and cider or beer. Often colonists half-heartedly obeyed the act by supplying fewer supplies than requested.

You may wish to check students' understanding of the topics as they prepare and present their minidramas.

Additional Background Information

The following are key understandings that should be included in the students' presentations of each topic.

1763 Proclamation of 1763   Prohibited settlement by colonists in lands gained after the French and Indian War, in which colonists had fought.

1764 Sugar Act   Added or increased taxes on sugar, textiles, coffee, iron, and other basic commodities to raise money to help the British pay for the French and Indian War.

1765 Quartering Act   Required colonists to provide food and lodging for British troops stationed in the colonies.

1765 Stamp Act   Imposed a tax by requiring purchase of special, stamped paper for all newspapers, pamphlets, legal documents, playing cards, etc.

1767 Townshend Acts   Placed small duties on everyday items such as tea, paper, lead, and glass.

1773 The Tea Act   Gave the British East India Company permission to lower the price of its tea below that of colonial merchants in order to increase sales and prevent bankruptcy.

1774 Intolerable/Coercive Acts   To punish Massachusetts for citizen protests, closed the port of Boston, suspended the Massachusetts charter, renewed the Quartering Act, and allowed British officials charged with crimes in America to be tried in England.

A Meeting of Minds
Exploring Theories of Government

About the Activity

Students should recognize that political leaders like Jefferson and Madison were not operating in a vacuum, but rather were deeply influenced by European political philosophers. In this activity, students explore the ideas of Machiavelli, Hobbes, Locke, and Rousseau that contributed to the American form of government.

After participating in the activity, students will be able to

- identify philosophies upon which framers of the Constitution drew.
- summarize key elements of the philosophies of Machiavelli, Hobbes, Locke, and Rousseau.
- apply political theories in considering a structure for a new form of government.

Planning for the Activity

Suggested Time: 2 class periods

Materials: Activity Sheets 5a–5d. For each sheet, make copies for one fourth of the students.

THE ACTIVITY

Getting Started

Begin by telling students that two fundamental questions facing American political thinkers in the late 1770s and 1780s were "who should rule?" and "why should others follow?" To answer these questions, they asked related questions, including "what is human nature?" and "what is the most effective form of government?"

Point out that these questions were difficult, but not new. Over the centuries many political thinkers had wrestled with them, including Niccolò Machiavelli, Thomas Hobbes, John Locke, and Jean Jacques Rousseau. American leaders studied the writings of these philosophers who preceded them.

Teaching

Explain that in this activity students will read fictitious interviews with four influential political philosophers. Each student will become an "expert" on the political ideas of one of these philosophers and then work with experts on the other three to make recommendations about the best form of government for the United States in 1787.

1. Divide students into four equal groups. Give each group copies of one activity sheet. Have them read the interview on their group's activity sheet to familiarize themselves with the thinking of their philosopher.

COMMENTS/NOTES

Background. The activity sheet interviews are a synthesis of the four philosophers' original writings and interpretations of their work in two books, *The Political Animal: Studies in Political Philosophy from Machiavelli to Marx*

2. Write the following questions on the chalkboard. Have each group decide how their philosopher would have answered them.

■ Why is government necessary?

■ What form of government is best? Why?

3. Organize students into four new groups, each composed of one expert on each of the four philosophers.

4. Explain that as experts on the theories of some great political thinkers, they have been asked to make recommendations to delegates preparing to attend the Constitutional Convention in 1787.

Instruct each group to develop a rationale for government and to make recommendations about the form the United States should adopt. In the group discussions, each expert should express the views of the philosopher he or she represents. Have each group appoint a recorder to summarize in writing the group's rationale and recommendations.

5. Call on each group to present its ideas to the class.

Concluding

After the group presentations, discuss the following questions:

■ Without government, do you think human beings would live in a "state of nature?"

■ In what ways did the philosophies of Machiavelli, Hobbes, Locke, and Rousseau influence American government?

Evaluating Student Work

Options for evaluation include:

■ evaluating participation in the large group introduction and conclusion activities. Criteria might include verbal contributions, quality of ideas presented, and attentiveness in listening.

■ evaluating participation in small groups. Criteria might include cooperation, expression of ideas, and attention to the task.

by Leo Rauch and *Modern Western Political Thought: Machiavelli to Marx* by Dante Germino.

_____

_____

_____

_____

_____

Background. Many of the delegates to the 1787 Constitutional Convention were familiar with the political ideas of Machiavelli, Hobbes, Locke, and Rousseau. For example, Jefferson had earlier included ideas from both Locke and Rousseau in the Declaration of Independence.

Encourage questions and gentle challenges from other "experts." If disagreements arise over interpretation of the philosophers' viewpoints, point out to students that scholars have disagreed about the positions of these philosophers for centuries.

_____

_____

_____

_____

_____

_____

_____

_____

_____

_____

_____

A Meeting of Minds
Hypothetical Interview with Niccolò Machiavelli

Interviewer: Please begin by telling our readers when and where you were born.

Machiavelli: I was born in 1469 in the Italian city of Florence.

Interviewer: Are you a political philosopher?

Machiavelli: I have written poetry, plays, short stories, and letters. My first love, however, is politics. In my book *The Prince* I teach my view of politics.

Interviewer: Why do you think government is necessary?

Machiavelli: People are never free of ambition; desire is endless. Because people desire but cannot get everything, their dissatisfaction is inevitable. This leads them into conflict, unless there is a stronger force to restrain them. Selfishness is such that a person will sooner forgive another for murdering his father than for depriving him of his inheritance. People will always be evil unless forced to do good.

Interviewer: What kind of "stronger force" do you propose?

Machiavelli: In *The Prince* I outline a plan for absolute rule in the form of one person—the prince. Because people are inclined to evil, the ruler must suppress them. The ruler must be all powerful and feared by the people. He must possess qualities of both a human being and a beast. As a beast, he should be both a fox and a lion: the fox can detect traps, as the lion cannot; the lion can frighten the wolves, as the fox cannot. He should strive to be a person of his word only when it is in his interest to do so. The ruler should seem to be merciful, faithful, humane, and religious, but he ought not to be so. Such characteristics limit a ruler and make him a danger to himself. He must know how not to be good.

Interviewer: Is it fair to say that you believe the end justifies the means?

Machiavelli: Yes. For the sake of a country's safety, there can be no reservations regarding an action or policy's justice or injustice, humanity or cruelty, honor or shame. The ultimate consideration can only be what will preserve the life and liberty of the country. We cannot ignore what people are and only consider what they ought to be. Only the strong ruler, possessing wisdom, stable judgment, and power, can curb the corruptness of human beings and maintain peace.

A Meeting of Minds
Hypothetical Interview with Thomas Hobbes

Interviewer: Please tell us where and when you were born.

Hobbes: I was born in 1588 in England. My mother gave birth to me upon hearing that the Spanish Armada was approaching England. In a way, it is as if my mother gave birth to twins: myself and fear.

Interviewer: Are you a political philosopher?

Hobbes: I am a political philosopher who draws from psychology and the new science of nature. I have written history, as well as about law and politics. My political philosophy is probably best presented in my book *Leviathan,* published in 1651.

Interviewer: Why is government necessary?

Hobbes: Without authority, human beings would live in a natural condition. In this condition, all persons have equal right to pursue the power, possessions, and resources necessary for a good life. Every person can use power to preserve life in any way deemed necessary. Every person's endless striving for power creates a predicament: people are necessarily drawn into competition. This leads to fighting and war, for the surest way to obtain power over a competitor is to kill, subdue, supplant, or repel the other person. Life in this state of nature is solitary, poor, nasty, brutish, and short!

Interviewer: What kind of government or political authority do you propose?

Hobbes: First, I want to talk about how government comes about. Human beings cannot long live in a state of anarchy and fear. The passion that moves people to leave this state of conflict and establish peace is the fear of violent death. This is the law of nature—a general rule, discovered by reason, which forbids a person to engage in self-destructive actions or to take away the means of preserving life. I prefer rule by a powerful monarch who creates conditions under which subjects can work and live in peace and harmony. The monarch must be strong and feared but also subject to the law of nature. If the monarch does not provide for peace, the people have a right to seek a new ruler.

Interviewer: By forming a peaceful society, do people give up rights?

Hobbes: People must give up the rights that brought them into conflict with others. Some force is needed, some sword, some person or persons standing outside the community to impose peace and compliance within the dictates of reason. People give up their rights and powers to this one person or sovereign assembly so that they, who by nature turn against each other, can become one society. Only in this way can the plurality of voices become one voice.

A Meeting of Minds
Hypothetical Interview with John Locke

Interviewer: Please begin by telling where and when you were born.

Locke: I was born in 1632 in England.

Interviewer: You are famous as a philosopher and a political philosopher.

Locke: Yes. Because I know your interest is in political philosophy, you would be best served to read my book *Two Treatises of Government.*

Interviewer: Why is government among people necessary?

Locke: By nature people are free. Reason, which is the law of nature, teaches people that because all are equal and independent, no one ought to harm another in life, health, liberty, or possessions. The law of nature obliges every person to act so as to preserve himself and others. A person has no right to another's person or possessions. A person can be secure in his own safety and possessions only so long as others recognize that they have no right to them.

The state of nature presents a problem, however. People are independent and equal, but also insecure because there is no authority to judge violations of nature's law and punish offenders. Each person is his own interpreter and enforcer of nature's law. Inevitably, each person is partial to his own case; people become blind to any interpretation of reason's law but their own and begin to act against the law. The state of nature is then transformed into a state of war.

Interviewer: What remedy do you suggest for this problem?

Locke: Being by nature free, equal, and independent, people cannot be subjugated to the political power of another. They must consent to unite into a community for comfortable, safe, and peaceful living. When any number of people have consented to make one community or government, they make one political body. In this body, the majority has a right to act.

Interviewer: You believe in government by majority rule then?

Locke: Yes. The majority must choose the type of government deemed most appropriate: a democracy, an oligarchy, or even a monarchy. The government chosen makes little difference because all governments are bound by trust put in them by people and the law of God and nature. Governments are obligated to (1) govern by established laws, (2) enact only laws necessary for the good of the people, (3) not raise taxes on property without the people's consent, given by themselves or their deputies, and (4) not transfer the power of making laws to anyone else or to place it anywhere but with the people.

A Meeting of Minds
Hypothetical Interview with Jean Jacques Rousseau

Interviewer: Please tell us where and when you were born.

Rousseau: I was born in Geneva in 1712.

Interviewer: You are said to be one of the great modern political writers.

Rousseau: You are very kind. My political arguments are best expressed in my book *The Social Contract*, published in 1762.

Interviewer: Why is government necessary?

Rousseau: Let me begin to answer the question by stating that the state of nature, as defined by Thomas Hobbes, no longer exists, perhaps never did, and probably never will exist. People are not basically selfish and evil. Although interested in self-preservation, they are basically compassionate and not the enemy of their kind. Government is necessary because people are born free, yet everywhere they are in chains. What I mean is that people are born free to do what their strength and liberty allow. This freedom results in a state of insecurity. To attain true freedom and stability, people must give up individual rights to the community. By agreement or contract, everyone gives up rights and no one gains power or advantage. Rights are given up not to a person or persons, but to the entire community, of which the individual is a part. Everyone gains the equivalent of what he loses and the increased force to conserve what he has. In giving himself to all, he gives himself to no one. Each of us puts his person and power under the supreme direction of the general will. Each member is an individual part of the whole.

Interviewer: What type of government do you think is best?

Rousseau: The social contract, or act of giving up individual power in favor of general will, creates a collective body that receives its unity, common ego, life, and will from this act. All participants are members of one body and function as a public person. Before, they were only individual persons. The general will is the interest of the community. Nothing may legitimately be done against that interest; otherwise a society ceases to be a community and becomes once again a mere collection of individuals. I believe that a democratic society or state, but not a democratic government, is best. The best government is one in which a few persons, under the control of the general will of the whole people, execute the laws and maintain civil and political liberty. Every society must have government, but there is no single form that is everywhere the best.

Power Plays: Delegated, Shared, Reserved
Advising Framers of the Constitution

About the Activity

What do Dr. Frankenstein and the framers of the Constitution have in common? In this activity, students consider the analogy between Frankenstein trying to form a living being without creating a monster and the framers trying to structure a strong federal government without overpowering state government.

After participating in the activity, students will be able to

- explain the terms *delegated, reserved,* and *shared powers* and give examples of such powers in the Constitution.
- use an analogy to explain the thinking of the framers in dividing powers between the federal and state governments.
- apply the concept of delegated, shared, and reserved powers to a present-day issue.

Planning the Activity

Suggested Time: 1 class period

Materials: Activity Sheet 6, one per student

Advance Preparation: This activity is based on an analogy of the creation of the Frankenstein monster and the framing of the Constitution. Before conducting the activity, familiarize yourself with the basic story from the *Frankenstein* novel. The book tells of a scientist, Victor Frankenstein, who seeks to create a living being for the good of humanity. Frankenstein learns the secret of infusing life into inanimate matter, but the being he creates becomes a monster who ultimately destroys him. Frankenstein's monster is imbued with many positive qualities, including great strength, intelligence, and obedience, but lacks the characteristics necessary to be accepted by others.

At first glance, the analogy might seem to trivialize the work of the Constitution's framers. However, records of the convention deliberations suggest that many delegates were, in fact, worried about creating an uncontrollable "monster." Such sentiments are expressed in the *Federalist Papers,* including Numbers 1, 2, and 51.

THE ACTIVITY

Getting Started

Call on volunteers to retell the story of Dr. Frankenstein and the monster he created in his laboratory. Direct students' attention away from the horror aspects of the story and toward the story's important themes: scientific experimentation, power, control, and the meaning of humanity.

Distribute copies of Activity Sheet 6. Group students in pairs and have them read the directions on the sheet and complete the questions on the *left side.* Emphasize that their task is to advise Dr. Frankenstein on creating a living being who will serve him without turning into a monster. Allow about 10 minutes for the pairs to work.

When students have completed their task, call on pairs to report their responses to each of the three questions.

COMMENTS/NOTES

Background. British author Mary Wollstonecraft Shelley published her novel *Frankenstein* in 1818.

Post their answers on the chalkboard and compare the recommendations of different pairs. Analyze the responses to help answer the following questions:

- How were the answers of various pairs alike and different?
- What kinds of controls were suggested to keep the creation from turning into an uncontrollable monster? Would the controls suggested be sufficient? Would you feel safe with such a being in your neighborhood?
- Would it be possible to come to a consensus among all class members about the best answers to each question?

Teaching

Explain to the class that the Constitutional Convention delegates, charged with creating a better structure of government for the new country, faced a challenge not unlike that of Dr. Frankenstein. Ask volunteers to suggest ways in which the framers' task was like Frankenstein's. Continue the discussion until the students recognize that the delegates to the Constitutional Convention desired to create a more powerful national government than that which had been structured by the Articles of Confederation. Yet they feared making a central government that was so powerful it would overwhelm the state governments.

1. Give students the following information, explaining that they will use it in completing their activity sheets.

The Constitution distinguishes three kinds of power: delegated, reserved, and shared. *Delegated powers* are those given specifically to the federal government. These include the powers to declare war, control international and interstate commerce, coin money, and conduct foreign relations. *Reserved powers* are powers the states keep for themselves. They include the power to regulate public health and morals, control intrastate trade, and ratify amendments to the Constitution. *Shared powers* are those that both the state and federal governments exercise. These include the power to tax, borrow money, and establish court systems.

2. Direct students to consider their answers to the Frankenstein monster questions, as well as the information you have just provided, when they answer, with their partners, the questions on the right side of the activity sheet. Emphasize that they should focus on one of the

In responding to the Frankenstein questions, students should be encouraged to combine creativity with realism. Seriously considering the questions will help students better understand the Constitution's division of powers.

Background. The following quotation from Thomas Jefferson suggests his concern about governments becoming too powerful: "Every government degenerates when trusted to the rulers of the people alone. The people themselves, therefore, are its only safe repositories."

24

central issues of the Constitutional Convention—how to create a national government that would be powerful enough to meet the needs of all the people but not so powerful that it would overwhelm state governments.

3. When students have finished, discuss the following questions to help them draw the analogy between the Frankenstein story and the framing of the Constitution.

- Which powers assigned to the monster could be identified as delegated, shared, and reserved?

- Of the powers assigned by the Constitution, which are delegated, shared, and reserved?

- Would your assignment of powers ensure the kind of creation Dr. Frankenstein wanted?

- How did the framers' assignment of powers affect the state and federal governments?

Concluding

Point out to students that the issue of the separation of powers between the federal and state governments is still alive today. Give the following example:

The power to set a legal age for drinking alcoholic beverages has traditionally been considered a concern of state governments because it relates to public health and safety, a state government responsibility. In the mid-1980s, most states had legal drinking ages of 18 or 19. Federal government officials, concerned about deaths caused from alcohol-impaired driving, proposed raising the legal drinking age to 21. However, some states objected and refused to change their laws, emphasizing that setting the legal age for drinking is a state power. To get around this impasse, the United States Congress passed a law withholding federal highway construction money from states that did not raise the legal drinking age to 21. The sums of money to be withheld were large, and states needed the funds in order to keep their highways in safe condition.

Direct students to write editorials on whether the federal government should withhold highway funds from states that refuse to raise the legal drinking age. In their editorials they are to show that the issue is a example of conflict between federal and state powers, take a position on whether the federal government should withhold funds, support their position with at least three arguments, and distribute a plan of action for states to follow in complying with or defying the federal law.

As students debrief the activity sheet, help them draw comparisons between Frankenstein's task in creating a living being and the framers' task in writing the Constitution. However, point out that while Frankenstein's creation became a monster, the structure of government in the United States has become a model many nations have studied.

25

Evaluating Student Work

Students' work in pairs and their editorials may both be used for assessment.

- Participation in pair discussions should be evaluated on an equal contribution by partners, attentiveness to the task, and arriving at supportable decisions.

- Editorials should be evaluated on their clarity in describing the issue of federal versus state powers, persuasiveness in stating and supporting reasons for or against federal involvement, and specificity in describing a logical course of action for states to take.

Power Plays: Delegated, Shared, Reserved
Assigning Powers

Directions

With a partner, you are to develop a plan for creating a Frankenstein-type monster. As you may recall from the story, Dr. Frankenstein sought to create a living being in the laboratory. However, he feared the experiment would become a monster if he did not retain control by limiting the being's traits and abilities.

Your task is to provide advice to Dr. Frankenstein on how to create his living being. Prepare by answering the three questions on the left. Consider how to make the creation powerful, but not so powerful that Dr. Frankenstein will not be able to control it. Explain each of your answers. Use additional paper as needed. You will be answering the questions on the right later.

The Frankenstein Monster

1. What human abilities and traits should the monster have? (example: breathing)

Our Government

1. What powers should the new federal government and the states share? (example: taxation)

2. What abilities or traits should be unique to the monster? (example: follows all orders)

2. What powers should be delegated only to the federal government? (example: power to coin money)

3. What human abilities or traits should not be given to the monster? (example: ability to show anger)

3. What powers should be reserved for the state governments? (example: ratification of amendments)

What limits, if any, would students be willing to place on the government's power to restrict individual freedoms? In this activity they answer that question with respect to a case in 1800, and then apply their reasoning to a recent situation.

After participating in the activity, students will be able to

- describe the basic elements of the Sedition Act of 1798.
- evaluate ways in which the Sedition Act might have been in conflict with the First Amendment protections of freedom of speech.
- evaluate and take a position on a case relating to the Sedition Act.
- identify similarities between events and actions that gave rise to the Sedition Act and current events.

Planning for the Activity

Suggested Time: 1–2 class periods

Materials: Activity Sheets 7a and 7b, one of each per student

THE ACTIVITY

Getting Started

Ask students to name the protections included in the First Amendment to the Constitution. Answers should include freedom of religion, speech, press, and assembly and the right to petition. Discuss which, if any, of the following actions would be protected under the First Amendment:

- writing an editorial criticizing the performance of Congress.
- printing a letter to the editor calling the President a fool and then criticizing a particular presidential policy.
- stating in a speech that a particular policy of the United States government is foolish.

Clarify that each of these actions, as stated, would be protected under provisions of the First Amendment. Ask the class if they think it is appropriate for such behaviors to be protected in a democracy like the United States.

Teaching

Explain that only seven years after the ratification of the Bill of Rights, a serious challenge was raised to First Amendment protections, especially freedom of speech. In

COMMENTS/NOTES

Background. The First Amendment reads: "Congress shall make no law respecting an establishment of religion or prohibiting the free exercise thereof, or abridging the freedom of speech or of the press or the right of the people peaceably to assemble and to petition the government for a redress of grievances."

a short lecture, provide the following information on the origins of this challenge:

- When John Adams was inaugurated President in 1797, tensions between France and the United States were already high. Adams and his fellow Federalists feared that excesses, such as the Reign of Terror, that had erupted during the French Revolution would incite similar acts in the United States.

- Only a few months after Adams's inauguration, American envoys to France were treated with disrespect and were told they would have to provide a "loan" (in fact, a bribe) in order to continue discussions with French Minister Talleyrand.

- To protect the nation against war with France, Adams moved to increase the size of the U.S. Navy, arm merchant ships, and obtain Congressional approval to increase the size of the regular army as well as to raise a provisional army of 10,000 soldiers. When news of the bribe, which became known as the XYZ Affair, reached the United States in 1798, Federalists voiced the rallying cry "Millions for defense, but not one cent for tribute." The ensuing period of tension between the U.S. and France was known as the "half war."

- American anger at France was not universal. Thomas Jefferson and many of his fellow Republicans admired the democratic spirit of the French and were opposed to many of the Federalists' actions.

- At the same time that Federalists and Republicans were disputing the country's relationship with France, the two parties were also in disagreement about the government's role at home. The Federalists tended to fear anarchy and stressed the duty of the federal government, in the form of a ruling elite, to control the people. The chief ends of government, according to Federalists, were political stability and security of the people. The Republicans, on the other hand, retained a faith in popular government. Fearing tyranny, they stressed liberty and the pursuit of happiness rather than authority and security.

- In this climate, in 1798, the Federalist-dominated Congress passed the four acts known as the Alien and Sedition Acts to restrict immigration, activities of foreigners in the United States, and criticism of the national government by citizens.

Background. Many Republicans, including Jefferson, had spent time in France and became acquainted with French leaders and thinkers.

Background. The Federalists saw real dangers in allowing unlimited free speech at a time when they feared that ideas of violent revolution might be imported into this nation. At the same time, the Republicans saw the actions of the Federalists as a potential move toward tyranny and the denial of individual freedoms.

Sedition can be defined as encouraging resistance to or insurrection against lawful authority.

1. Distribute Activity Sheet 7a and ask students for an initial opinion on whether the Sedition Act seems to comply with the provisions of the First Amendment. Review the three actions discussed in the "Getting Started" section and determine whether each would be allowed under the Sedition Act.

2. Explain that students will have a chance to apply their understanding of the First Amendment and the Sedition Act to an historical case. Distribute Activity Sheet 7b on the Charles Holt case. Allow time for each student to decide whether Holt's action should have been considered protected under the First Amendment.

3. Form small groups of three to five students. Direct group members to compare their opinions on the Holt case and to identify at least two reasons for and two against regarding his action as protected by the First Amendment. Remind the groups to be prepared to explain their reasons, based on information in the activity sheet.

4. In a class discussion, compare the conclusions of the small groups. On the chalkboard write two headings: *Protected* and *Not Protected*. Under them list specific reasons identified by the groups.

Arguments for regarding Holt's action as unprotected should establish that the Sedition Act itself did not contradict the First Amendment's intent—that freedom of speech must sometimes be limited to maintain order and national security. Holt's action could be seen as undermining public support for a federal army in a time of crisis and presenting an intentionally false statement about the "standing army." As such, it could be said to violate both the letter of the Sedition Act and the spirit of the First Amendment.

Arguments for considering Holt's action protected by the First Amendment might claim that the letter simply stated a political opinion on a subject of legitimate public debate and as such did not threaten national security. Also, using the phrase "standing army" could be seen as a reasonable interpretation, not a deliberate or malicious falsehood. The constitutionality of the Sedition Act could be questioned on the grounds that the terms "scandalous" and "malicious" are so vague as to stifle political debate and threaten democracy itself.

Concluding

Tell the class that on April 12, 1800, a jury found Charles Holt guilty of violating the Sedition Act. At his sentencing, the judge lectured Holt, declaring that "libels on a

Point out to students that after being challenged by two state governments, the Sedition Act expired in 1801 and was not reenacted.

free government have (a tendency) to discredit and destroy the Government itself." Then he imposed a three-month prison sentence and a $200 fine.

Ask students whether they agree with the decision, using the following questions in a final discussion:

- Which arguments in support of Holt were most persuasive?

- Which arguments against Holt were strongest?

- Why do you think Holt, rather than the writer of the letter, was prosecuted?

- Do you think the Sedition Act was constitutional? Why or why not?

- What rights should the government have to limit freedom of speech and the press in times of war? Should the same limits apply when there is only the threat of war, as was the case in 1798?

- How should a democracy balance the government's need to protect the security of citizens and citizens' rights to free expression?

As a final assignment, direct students to write a closing statement to the jury for either the prosecution or the defense attorney in the Charles Holt case. In their statements, they should summarize the facts of the case and argue for or against Holt. The statements must be based on careful reasoning and include persuasive arguments.

Evaluating Student Work

Students may be evaluated on both their participation in group work and their final written assignment using the following criteria:

- active cooperation in small group discussion.

- statements that accurately state the facts of the case, clearly identify the position being advocated, persuasively state reasons for the position, and appropriately refer to the First Amendment and the Sedition Act.

Limiting Freedom: The Sedition Act
Excerpts from the Sedition Act

The Sedition Act
"An Act for the punishment of certain crimes against the United States"

Section 1. *Be it enacted by the Senate and House of Representatives of the United States of America, in Congress assembled,* That . . . if any person or persons . . . shall counsel, advise or attempt to procure any insurrection, riot, unlawful assembly, or combination, whether such conspiracy, threatening, counsel, advice, or attempt shall have the proposed effect or not, he or they shall be deemed guilty of a high misdemeanor, and on conviction, before any court of the United States . . . shall be punished during a term not less than six months nor exceeding five years . . .

Section 2. *And be it further enacted,* that if any person shall write, print, utter or publish, or shall cause or procure to be written, printed, uttered or published, or shall knowingly and willingly assist or aid in writing, printing, uttering or publishing any false, scandalous and malicious writing or writings against the government of the United States or either house of the Congress of the United States, or the President of the United States, with intent to defame the said government or . . . to excite against them . . . the hatred of the good people of the United States, or to stir up sedition within the United States, or to excite any unlawful combinations therein, for opposing or resisting any law of the United States, or any act of the President of the United States . . . [that person] shall be punished by a fine not exceeding two thousand dollars, and by imprisonment not exceeding two years.

Limiting Freedom: The Sedition Act
Analyzing a Charge of Sedition

Directions

After carefully reading the case of Charles Holt, decide whether you think Holt's action was protected by the First Amendment. Give at least one reason in support of your decision. Be prepared to compare your reasoning with others in a small group discussion.

The Case of Charles Holt

Charles Holt edited the New London *Bee* from 1797–1802 in New London, Connecticut. During its brief existence, the *Bee* was said to have provided more information per issue on political matters than any other Connecticut newspaper. However, it had the misfortune of being the most Republican newspaper in Connecticut, which had the strongest Federalist party of any state. Despite Federalist contempt for both the Bee and its editor, Holt stood his ground. He stated, "Whatever may serve the true republican interest and support the wholesome laws and constitution of my country shall be my constant endeavor to collect and publish."

Holt, like most Republicans, opposed the creation of the Provisional Army that was raised during the Half War with France. On May 8, 1799, he printed a letter from a reader who condemned the federal forces as a standing army. The letter writer also made strong remarks about the character of Alexander Hamilton, who had confessed to adultery. Was this a man, he asked, who should stand as a model for American youth? Federalist presses, the letter writer charged, had screened this information from the citizens of Connecticut. He urged Connecticut's citizens to consider carefully whether they should permit their sons to join this military force and fight in wars that might destroy "both you and them."

Several Federalist newspapers pointed out this letter to the federal district attorney in Connecticut, who convened a grand jury to decide whether to charge Holt with violating the Sedition Act. On September 17, 1799, this grand jury charged Holt with sedition based on the issue of the *Bee* that contained the letter to the editor. The grand jury accused Holt of stirring up discontent and sedition among the citizenry, with intent to defame the government. The letter, the grand jury charged, was designed to excite an unlawful opposition to the army recruiting service. Holt was arrested on September 21, pleaded not guilty, and went to trial in April, 1800.

Holt's lawyers attacked the constitutionality of the Sedition Act and argued that the factual parts of the letter were true. Other parts, they claimed, did not violate the law because they were only opinion. The prosecutor argued that Holt had published a falsehood because the letter called the army a "standing force" rather than a "provisional force." According to the prosecutor, this undermined citizens' confidence in the government. He concluded by saying that the only liberty taken away from Holt by the Sedition Act was "the liberty of lying maliciously—a liberty which none but rascals can wish to enjoy."

About the Activity

After studying descriptions of transportation in primary sources and fiction, students create projects to illustrate both the romantic and unromantic aspects of travel in the early and mid 1800s.

After participating in the activity, students will be able to

- identify forms of transportation in the early and mid 1800s.
- recognize the benefits and problems created by the expansion of transportation systems after the early 1800s.
- explain why transportation was a theme in the works of artists, writers, and musicians.

Planning for the Activity

Suggested Time: 2 class periods

Materials: Activity Sheets 8a and 8b, one of each per student

THE ACTIVITY

Getting Started

Ask students why transportation was an important issue to the growing nation in the early 1800s. What kinds of water and land transportation were available? Write *Water Transportation* on the chalkboard and ask students for examples. (Answers may include such vessels as canoes, steamboats, paddlewheelers, ferries, and canal barges.) Write *Overland Transportation* on the chalkboard and ask for examples. (Answers may include walking, horses, wagons, carriages, and stagecoaches. Students should note that the locomotive was only in its infancy.)

Teaching

Note that people in the early to mid 1800s were fascinated with transportation because it offered access to the potential riches of lands to the west. The fascination was reflected in art, songs, poems, fiction, newspapers, and cartoons.

1. Distribute copies of Activity Sheet 8a. Ask what impressions of river travel are suggested by the song, ad, and cartoon.

2. Distribute Activity Sheet 8b. Read the selection aloud and ask students what impression of river travel the reading offers.

3. Assign students to create a song, poem, poster, cartoon, or story about a form of transportation common to

COMMENTS/NOTES

_____

_____

_____

_____

_____

_____

_____

_____

_____

_____

_____

_____

Background. "Low Bridge, Everybody Down" was originally a song about travel on the Erie Canal. Canal boats were pulled by horses or mules that walked on towpaths and were driven by men called *boggies.* Boggies issued warnings to passengers to lower their heads as the boat approached a bridge.

Activity Sheet 8b provides an example of a fictional account based on historical research. The description of the

the period. They may choose from any form listed on the chalkboard or one they identify from research.

4. Direct students to rely on information from their text and other classroom or library resources. Their projects should be accurate and creative, and make a significant point about the transportation of the period.

Concluding

Have students share projects with the class. After each presentation, ask the presenter to cite one piece of new information about early transportation that he or she learned.

Conclude by discussing these questions:

- What benefits did expanded systems of transportation provide in the 1800s?
- What problems did they create?
- How does our continuing expansion of transportation systems help our country today? What problems have resulted?
- Is transportation still a theme of art, literature, and music? What examples can you name?

Evaluating Student Work

Options for assessment include:

- evaluating participation in the introductory and concluding discussions. Criteria might include amount of contribution, quality of ideas, and active listening.
- evaluating projects. Criteria might include accuracy, originality, quality of work, demonstration of ideas, and effort.

flatboat trip was researched and written by Ron Schukar, one of the *Active Learning* authors. Suggest that students locate resource materials by looking first in the card or computer catalogue under the headings *Transportation in the United States* and *United States History, 1800 to 1850.* From those general headings, they will be able to identify more specific topics.

To conserve class time, you might assign the projects as homework.

Background. Remind students that although President Madison emphasized to Congress that he wanted to create a national transportation system, when a transportation bill passed Congress after great debate, he vetoed it. Madison had concluded that the Constitution did not permit government financing of such construction.

Discuss with students the role of the federal government today in financing the country's interstate highway system.

_____

_____

Challenge students as they read upcoming chapters in their text to look for forms of transportation that were invented or became widely used during the remainder of the nineteenth century and into the twentieth century.

_____

_____

_____

Setting a Nation in Motion
Transportation in Primary Sources

Low Bridge, Everybody Down

I've got a mule and her name is Sal,
Fifteen miles on the Erie Canal.
She's a good worker and a good old pal,
Fifteen miles on the Erie Canal.
We've hauled some barges in our day,
Filled with lumber, coal, and hay,
And we know every inch of the way
From Albany to Buffalo.

Chorus:
Low bridge! Everybody down!
Low bridge! We're a-coming to a town.
You'll always know your neighbor,
    you'll always know your pal,
If you've ever navigated on the Erie Canal.

We'd better get on our way, old pal,
Fifteen miles on the Erie Canal.
You can bet your life I'd never part with Sal,
Fifteen miles on the Erie Canal.
Get us there, Sal, here comes a lock;
We'll make Rome 'fore six o'clock.
One more trip and back we'll go,
Right back home to Buffalo.

A NEW BERTH.
Candid Landlady. "THE FIRST FROM THE TOP, SIR, IS THE ONLY BED VACANT; BUT YOU HAVE GOT VERY NICE NEIGHBORS—ONE GENTLEMAN CHEWS, BUT THE OTHERS ONLY SMOKE!"

FERRY.
The subscriber has prepared himself with a first rate **FERRY BOAT,** WITH APRONS AND BANNISTERS. At his Ferry opposite Market street, Vincennes, immediately on the road to St. Louis, where, by his strict attention and care, he flatters himself all who may wish to cross the Wabash will be accommodated to their satisfaction.

October 11th, 1823.   JAMES NABB.

Setting a Nation in Motion
Transportation in Fiction

Background

The following is a fictional account of life aboard a flatboat that traveled along the Mississippi River from Memphis, Tennessee, to Natchez, Mississippi.

On a Flatboat to Natchez

In July of 1817, Captain Jedediah Hawke, a seasoned flatboat operator and legend among river haulers, offered me passage from my home in Memphis to the community of Natchez. "Boy," Hawke said, "You gotta earn your way down south on this here ol' boat. There ain't no free riden', ya hear? You jump on board, you become one of Hawke's hands."

So it was. Needing to get to Natchez to see my sister and her husband before they journeyed west, I jumped on board. For the next twelve days, I was one of Hawke's hands. I think Hawke thought I was his "left" hand. On this particular trip, Hawke's boat was loaded with livestock. Individuals and families in Natchez were waiting for the livestock to arrive so that they could begin their journey west. Captain Hawke said that one of the horses on board was sold to my brother-in-law. For twelve days, I lived with the animals. The fowl fluttered, cattle lowed, horses trampled, turkeys gobbled, and dogs barked—constantly. It was a most unpleasant experience for the son of a storekeep and everyday resident of a house in the city.

Other boats on the river were loaded with whiskey, tobacco, cotton, corn, furniture, and tools. All destined for the west by the Red River, which joined the Mississippi at Natchez. I noticed that most of the other boats took the opportunity to avoid Hawke's boat. Those that glided by us often signaled that our boat possessed a unique aroma. The crew felt guilty by association.

During the twelve days I was on board Hawke's boat, the crew went to shore twice. These short overnight stays allowed crews of the flatboats to eat, drink, and be merry. The village people, as you can imagine, love and hate the crews. I am told that during the stop-overs, as they are called, children are not allowed on the street until dawn, when once again the crews and boats get underway.

The flatboats travel silently and smoothly down the tree-lined river. Sometimes the only sound is that of the dogs. I am sure that on a boat loaded with coal or lumber, there are times when no sound is heard for hours. The flatboats serve an important function. Able to negotiate shallow water when necessary, they move people and the goods so desperately needed in the western settlements. I feel, as I sit on the top of the boat in the sun, that for these few short days, smell and inconvenience aside, I am playing a small but significant role in the history of this new nation. There are people waiting to take these animals west. They depend on me, much as I depend on the butcher or baker back in Memphis.

Wrestling with the Issue of Slavery
Participating in Paired Writing

About the Activity

No national debate has been fiercer than the one over slavery. In this activity pairs of students engage in written dialogues to come to a better understanding of proslavery and antislavery arguments.

After participating in the activity, students will be able to

- identify proslavery and antislavery arguments.
- conduct a debate through paired writing.

Planning for the Activity

Suggested Time: 2 class periods

Materials: Activity Sheet 9, one copy per student

Advance Preparation: Accumulate resources on proslavery and antislavery arguments for use in the classroom.

THE ACTIVITY

Getting Started

Point out that today slavery has been almost universally condemned and outlawed. Tell students that modern governments have agreed that it is morally wrong for one person to enslave another. Call on volunteers to cite reasons why slavery is wrong and post their responses on the chalkboard.

Teaching

Explain that in this activity students will debate the institution of slavery as it was practiced in the United States before the Civil War. The format they will use is a *paired writing*—a written dialogue in which partners take opposing points of view on an issue and then present their positions through a series of arguments and rebuttals.

1. To prepare students for the paired writing, have them list proslavery and antislavery arguments, using their texts and other resources as necessary.

2. Begin the next class period by writing the headings *Proslavery* and *Antislavery* on the chalkboard and calling on students to identify arguments they found in their research. Clarify arguments and write them under the appropriate headings.

3. Divide the class into two large groups and have the groups move to opposite sides of the room. Assign one group to represent the proslavery position and the other the antislavery position. Allow time for members of each group to discuss and decide on the strongest arguments

COMMENTS/NOTES

for their position and the potentially strongest rebuttals to their arguments.

4. Distribute copies of Activity Sheet 9, read the directions with students, and answer any questions. Emphasize that the paired writing task requires each pair to produce a *continuous written* dialogue by passing their paper back and forth according to the steps described on the activity sheet.

5. Identify pairs of students, with one proslavery and one antislavery partner in each pair, but have students remain with their large groups on opposite sides of the room.

6. Begin the paired writing by having members of the proslavery group write introductory paragraphs. Adhere to the four-minute time limit.

7. At the end of four minutes, direct the proslavery partners to deliver their paragraphs to their antislavery partners. Notify the antislavery partners that they are beginning Round 2, during which they will have four minutes to write their introductory statements.

8. Continue following the directions on the activity sheet until all eight rounds have been completed.

Concluding

Debrief the activity by asking students to identify the arguments on both sides of the issue that they thought were most compelling, and discuss why these arguments were persuasive. Call on proslavery partners to discuss what it was like for them to argue in support of a practice that has been universally rejected. Ask what they learned from playing this role. Challenge students to keep arguments on both sides in mind as they continue to study the tensions between the North and the South.

Evaluating Student Work

The written dialogues can be used as the primary source of evaluation for this activity. Criteria for assessment may include accuracy of arguments presented, preciseness of rebuttals, and clarity of introductory and concluding statements. Students may be graded as a pair or individually.

If the class has an odd number of students, you may choose to serve as a partner for one student, or have one group of three students.

Emphasize that "proslavery" students are representing a point of view that was once widely held in the United States. Students are not expected to accept the proslavery arguments but are to represent the position credibly in the dialogue.

Monitor the nonwriting group during the early rounds to make certain students use their time to prepare for the next round.

Because the activity probably cannot be completed in one class period, you may wish to have students complete the first two rounds during one class and resume with Round 3 the next period. Have students leave their papers in the classroom overnight.

Adjust the writing times to meet the abilities of your students. You might permit students with insufficient writing skills to tape-record their responses.

Additional Background Information

Before the Civil War, some proslavery advocates argued that slavery was actually a benefit to captive Africans because it "civilized" them by putting them into contact with the "superior" white race. References to slavery in the Bible were used to support this position. Proslavery proponents also maintained that slaves were not as deprived as some people suggested, because owners had a moral obligation to provide slaves with housing, food, and employment. This argument compared the lives of southern slaves with the lives of northern "wage slaves," who had none of the "amenities" of southern slaves. Cruel treatment of slaves was acknowledged by defenders of slavery, but only as an exception to the generally "positive" treatment slaves received. Finally, those who supported the institution of slavery claimed that it was essential to the economy of the South.

Abolitionists and antislavery activists countered proslavery arguments by maintaining that it was morally wrong for any one person to hold another in bondage and to deny that person the most basic freedoms. Slavery was also seen as having negative economic effects on the South because it eliminated the need to develop a true working class and to create productive capital. Cruel treatment of slaves was cited, including the practice of breaking up families and selling children away from their parents. It was argued that, unlike southern slaves, northern wage earners had the opportunity, even if slight, to better their lot through hard work and saving. Finally, northerners objected that the three-fifths rule of counting slaves in the census gave southern states an unfairly large number of representatives in the House of Representatives.

Wrestling with the Issue of Slavery
Participating in Paired Writing

Directions

In this activity, you will be doing paired writing—a written dialogue with a partner. One of you will represent the proslavery viewpoint, and the other will argue the antislavery position. Here is the dialogue format:

Round	Task	Writing Time
1.	Proslavery partner writes an introductory proslavery statement (1–2 paragraphs)	4 minutes
2.	Antislavery partner writes an introductory antislavery statement (1–2 paragraphs)	4 minutes
3.	Proslavery partner writes one proslavery argument (1 paragraph)	4 minutes
4.	Antislavery partner writes a rebuttal to the previous proslavery argument (1 paragraph) and writes one antislavery argument (1 paragraph)	8 minutes
5.	Proslavery partner writes a rebuttal to previous antislavery argument (1 paragraph) and writes one proslavery argument (1 paragraph)	8 minutes
6.	Antislavery partner writes a rebuttal to previous proslavery argument (1 paragraph) and writes one antislavery argument (1 paragraph)	8 minutes
7.	Proslavery partner writes a rebuttal to the previous antislavery argument (1 paragraph) and writes a concluding proslavery statement (1 paragraph)	6 minutes
8.	Antislavery partner writes a concluding statement (1 paragraph)	3 minutes

Begin at the top of a sheet of paper and continue on additional paper as needed. While your partner is writing, you should prepare for your next task. Plan your arguments and try to anticipate the rebuttals of your partner. Your paper will be evaluated on the clarity, accuracy, and strength of both the arguments and rebuttals.

War with Mexico?
Debating a Declaration of War

About the Activity

What questions raised during conflicts between Mexico and the United States in the early 1800s are still being asked in international relations? In this activity, students consider the issues surrounding the Mexican-American War and the general question of when a country is justified in going to war. This activity may introduce or conclude a study of the Mexican-American War, but should not be initiated until students have studied the formation of Texas as an independent republic.

After participating in the activity, students will be able to

- describe the historical context of the Mexican-American War.
- identify reasons for and against the declaration of war against Mexico.
- defend a position on the appropriateness of going to war with Mexico.

Planning for the Activity

Suggested Time: 1 class period

Materials: Activity Sheet 10, one copy per student

THE ACTIVITY

Getting Started

Begin by asking students to suggest reasons why one country might go to war against another. List their answers on the chalkboard. Challenge students to cite historical examples of wars that have started for the reasons listed. Ask them to review the reasons and discuss whether some might be more compelling or justifiable than others, and why.

Teaching

Explain that in this activity students will examine the reasons why the United States went to war with Mexico in 1846. If the class has not studied events leading up to the Mexican-American War, review the information in the "Additional Background Information" that follows these directions.

1. Distribute copies of Activity Sheet 10. Have students read the information and write their answers to the question at the end of the reading.

2. When all students have finished writing their opinions on whether war should have been declared against Mexico, have them indicate with a show of hands which ones responded "yes" and which responded "no."

3. Form small groups of students who responded "yes" and other small groups of students who responded "no."

COMMENTS/NOTES

Reasons for going to war might include protecting access to natural resources (Persian Gulf War), protecting American lives (military action in Grenada and Panama), protecting basic American values and ways of life (World War II).

Background. During the first half of the 1800s, the area of the United States expanded from the original thirteen states and the Northwest Territory to include all of today's contiguous 48 states. Territory was acquired through treaty, purchase, annexation, and war. Expansionism was often justified by the concept of manifest destiny. (See "Additional Background Information.")

Background. Philosopher and writer Henry David Thoreau criticized the decision to go to war against Mexico. Based on his beliefs, Thoreau refused to pay taxes as a means of protest and spent time in jail for his actions. His writings on civil disobedience came from this time period.

Direct each group to spend 10 minutes sharing and brainstorming arguments to support their response. Encourage students to use information from the activity sheet, text, and other sources to which they have access.

4. Write the headings *Arguments For Declaring War* and *Arguments Against Declaring War* on the chalkboard. Call on students from each small group to give reasons for their position. List the reasons on the board.

Concluding

Lead a class discussion of which arguments for and against declaring war are most persuasive. Then ask the following questions:

- What actions, if any, might have prevented the war? Explain.
- Polk blamed the war on "the act of Mexico herself." How do you think Mexican leaders would have responded to his claim?
- What role did the belief in manifest destiny play in United States actions?
- Under what circumstances does a country have a right to declare war on another country?

Assign students to write a one-page position paper explaining why they would or would not have supported a declaration of war. Emphasize that the papers should include evidence and well-reasoned arguments based on information in the activity sheet and in other sources they may consult.

Evaluating Student Work

Students may be assessed on both their participation in the small group and class discussions and on their position paper. Use the following criteria.

- Discussion participation should include attentiveness to the information in the activity sheet, thoughtful contributions, and active listening.
- Position papers should reflect accurately factual information, take a clear stand, support the stand with well-reasoned arguments, and use appropriate language and writing style.

Arguments for declaring war might include that Mexico was unwilling to negotiate, that American blood was shed on "American" soil, that territorial expansion was desirable and inevitable, and that Mexico was not meeting its financial obligations to United States citizens.

As an alternative to writing a position paper, students could be assigned to read Thoreau's essay "Civil Disobedience" and report on its implications for American involvement in the Mexican-American War.

Arguments against declaring war might include that manifest destiny was morally wrong and culturally arrogant, that the United States had not respected Mexico's national pride, that the movement of United States troops into the disputed territory was provocative, and that the United States had no right to claim land controlled by another nation.

_____

_____

_____

_____

Additional Background Information

Manifest destiny is an extension of a concept sometimes called *civil religion*. Since the early days of the American Revolution, the notion that the United States has the obligation, both collective and individual, to carry out God's will on earth has been strongly evident. American civil religion derives its symbols from Christianity but is not itself a form of Christianity. There is no mention of Christ, but frequent mention of God. Civil religion allows individuals to hold whatever personal religious beliefs they wish. Echoes of civil religion can still be heard today in pronouncements by Presidents and other leaders.

Manifest destiny, an extension of civil religion, was a popular justification for United States territorial expansion. Many Americans believed that the United States had a special destiny, given by God, to take control of the continent and spread the benefits of American democracy and values. However, actions taken in the name of manifest destiny often reflected racism and attitudes of cultural superiority. Europeans, Mexicans and, in particular, Native Americans were generally viewed as an obstacle to be overcome in the drive to achieve the rapid and "orderly" settlement of new territory.

Among the many motivations that contributed to the declaration of war on Mexico, the belief in manifest destiny played an important role. For example, the United States wanted to gain control of the Mexican province of California, not only because California's ports would be of great commercial value, but also because annexation would fulfill expansionists' dreams of a nation from "sea to shining sea."

War with Mexico?
Taking a Position

During the early to mid 1800s, the United States was in a period of territorial expansion and several times showed a willingness to go to war over disputed territories. For example, in 1845, during the presidency of James Polk, the country threatened war with Britain to obtain the Oregon Territory. In the southwestern United States, several issues had been creating tensions since 1836, when Texas won its independence from Mexico. One problem was the attitude of the two nations. Mexico was a young and proud republic. The United States, also young, was caught up in the spirit of manifest destiny.

A second problem arose in 1845, when the United States agreed to annex Texas and admit it to the Union as a new state. Mexico declared the annexation a clear act of aggression and cut diplomatic relations. The fact that the Mexican government had not repaid financial claims of United States citizens and other foreigners, stemming from Mexico's 1821 war of independence from Spain, created a third problem.

The fourth major issue involved a disputed boundary between Mexico and Texas. The traditional boundary had been the Nueces River, but Texas claimed that the new boundary should be the Rio Grande, which would cost Mexico several hundred square miles of territory.

President Polk's desire to increase the territory of the United States was well known. In fact, he had once told friends that he dreamed of adding the Mexican territories of New Mexico and California to the United States. In 1845 he sent a diplomat, John Slidell, to Mexico to discuss the Texas boundary dispute and to offer $30 million for California and New Mexico. Still enraged over the Texas annexation, Mexico refused to negotiate.

In 1846, with negotiations stalled, Polk sent troops under the leadership of General Zachary Taylor into the disputed territory across the Nueces River, east of the Rio Grande. In explaining his actions, Polk said, "Nothing can remain but to take the redress of the injuries to our citizens and the insults to our government in our own hands." Mexico considered the action an invasion of Mexican territory. In late April 1846, Mexican troops attacked Taylor's troops, inflicting some casualties.

On May 11 President Polk asked Congress to declare war on Mexico, saying, "Mexico has passed the boundary of the United States, has invaded our territory and shed American blood upon the American soil. . . . As war exists, and, notwithstanding all our efforts to avoid it, exists by the act of Mexico herself . . . I [ask] Congress to recognize the existence of war."

If you were a member of Congress in 1846, would you have voted to declare war? Why or why not?

Directions: On the back of this sheet, answer the question above, stating at least two reasons for your answer. Be prepared to discuss your opinion with others.

Making It Faster
Simulating Craft and Mass Production

About the Activity

As students study the mid 1800s, when the Industrial Revolution was well under way, this activity provides a quick but powerful simulation of the impact of mass production. Students apply both craft and mass production methods in constructing chains made of paper links, and then compare the results.

After participating in the activity, students will be able to

- compare the efficiency of individual-craft and mass production.
- identify advantages and disadvantages of craft labor and mass production.
- evaluate the impact of mass production on national industrial growth and on the lives of working people.

Planning for the Activity

Suggested Time: 1 class period

Materials: $8\frac{1}{2} \times 11$" white paper, one ream; about 20 rulers; about 20 scissors; staplers, gluesticks, and/or tape dispensers totalling about 20.

Advance Preparation: Prepare a sample chain, with each link measuring 1" × 10".

THE ACTIVITY

Getting Started

Begin by asking students why they think mass production increasingly replaced craft work. (Students may note greater output and savings in time and money.) Then tell them that they will be testing both methods by creating paper chains in an allotted 20 minutes.

Teaching

Demonstrate the steps of measuring and cutting strips, forming links, and fastening links (using glue, tape, or staples). Show the sample chain, and on the chalkboard post the standard measurement of each link: 1" × 10".

1. Direct two thirds of the class to gather on one side of the room. Explain that each person in this group is to create his or her own chain.

2. Allow five minutes for the remaining one third to divide the steps among themselves to create a mass production arrangement. This group will create a single chain.

3. Make sure that each group has enough supplies so that no one is slowed by waiting for materials. Stress that the goal is to create as long a chain as possible in 20 minutes. Then signal for the students to begin.

COMMENTS/NOTES

Background. Most historians date the beginning of mass production in the United States from 1800. In 1798 the United States government contracted with inventor Eli Whitney to make 10,000 muskets in two years. Whitney spent the two years developing the techniques of manufacturing interchangeable parts, the concept upon which mass production is based. Although he delivered only 500 muskets in 1800, his mass production operation was in place, and the remaining guns were soon to come.

The impact of mass production was felt most significantly during the rapid industrial growth of the late 1800s and early 1900s. By the mid 1800s, though, the growth of northern factories had already reinforced the distinction between an industrial North and an agrarian South. This contrast was a factor in the sectionalism leading up to the Civil War.

4. After 20 minutes ask the individual workers to note the number in their group, to count the total number of links in their chains, and to calculate the average number of links per worker. Have the mass production group do the same. Write "Craft Production" and "Mass Production" on the chalkboard. Under each heading write:

Total Workers   ____

Total Links   ____

Average Links
per Worker   ____

Post all the results. Which method produced more links? More links per worker?

Concluding

Ask the following questions to help students reflect on the simulation:

- How did the two methods differ?
- What were advantages/disadvantages of each?
- What made one method more productive?
- Which workers had greater independence?
- What risks existed in mass production that did not exist for individual workers?

Direct students to write two or three paragraphs explaining why, if they were a worker in the mid 1800s, they would rather be an individual craft worker or a factory worker. Challenge them to note the pros and cons of their choices.

Evaluating Student Work

Assessment may be based on the following criteria.

- Participation in the simulation should reflect attention to the task and serious reflection on the experience.
- Written work should clearly identify mass production advantages (such as greater volume and less reliance on individual abilities) and disadvantages (such as harsh working conditions, loss of workers' pride, stifled creativity).

Encourage students to reread their paragraphs after they have finished studying the impact of the Industrial Revolution in the 1800s and early 1900s. Ask them if they would change their answers after their study.

Why the Civil War?
Depicting Causes in Movie Posters

About the Activity

Can students distinguish between various historians' interpretations of the causes of the Civil War? In this activity, they show their understanding of five interpretations by creating movie posters.

After participating in this activity, students will be able to

- ■ distinguish between five interpretations of the causes of the Civil War.
- ■ depict one interpretation in a movie-poster format.

Planning for the Activity

Suggested Time: 1 to 2 class periods

Materials: Activity Sheets 12a through 12e, enough copies of each sheet for one fifth of students; five sheets of poster paper; color markers or pencils

Advance Preparation: To stimulate students' creativity, you may wish to bring to class movie advertisement clippings. Most advertisements are based on the posters created for theater display.

THE ACTIVITY

Getting Started

Explain that historians have long debated the causes of the Civil War. Divide the class into five groups, and assign each a different activity sheet. Tell students to complete individually the reading and questions on their sheets.

Teaching

When students have completed the activity sheets, conduct a class discussion.

1. Call on a member of each group to summarize the viewpoint of that group's reading. Help students summarize the differing viewpoints on the major cause of the Civil War: Rhodes (12a)—slavery; Owsley (12b)—economic differences; Randall (12c)—fanaticism, misunderstanding, misrepresentation, or politics; Schlesinger (12d)—moral differences; Potter (12e)—misconceptions about each other's society. Make certain they have a clear understanding not only of the differences but also of the ways the interpretations overlap.

2. Ask each group to imagine their reading is to be the basis of a movie about the major cause of the Civil War. Their first task is to create a storyline for the movie, give it a powerful title, identify major roles, and name principal stars.

COMMENTS/NOTES

To conserve class time, assign the activity sheet to be completed as homework. If the readings are difficult for some students, you may wish to have students discuss them in groups before answering the questions individually.

Background. Official explanations of the Civil War's causes began with summaries of events leading to the war that President Abraham Lincoln and President Jefferson Davis gave to their respective congresses.

Background. For information about the authors of the selections on the activity sheets, see "Additional Background Information."

3. Once they have completed the first part, tell them that the second task is for each group to create a poster advertising the movie they have conceptualized. Show the advertisements you collected and call on volunteers to describe other effective posters they can recall.

4. Read or post the following poster criteria:

- a powerful, descriptive title
- text and visuals that clearly communicate the cause expressed by the author of your reading
- identification of principal stars
- use of movie poster style: clear lettering, interesting pictures, color illustration

Provide paper and drawing supplies. Have students refer to their text and other resources, as well as their activity sheet. Stress that all group members must actively participate in creating the poster. Members' names and functions should be listed on the poster.

Concluding

Display the posters and have representatives from each group explain how their poster illustrates a cause of the Civil War. Conclude by discussing these questions:

- Is any interpretation more accurate or compelling than the others? Explain.
- Are there other explanations of the Civil War that we should consider?
- Why have historians disagreed on the major causes of the Civil War? Are there more recent events on which historians disagree?
- What do you think was the most significant cause of the Civil War?

Evaluating Student Work

Student work may be evaluated on participation in creating the posters and on the posters themselves. Participation in group work can be assessed on attentiveness to the task, willingness to assume responsibility, and understanding of the group's design concept. The posters should be evaluated on the criteria listed in #4, above.

As an example, a film representing sectionalism as the primary cause of the Civil War might be entitled "Irreconcilable Differences," and its poster might include images illustrating economic and social contrasts between the prewar North and South.

Remind students that all members of the group have shared responsibility, meaning that no one member is finished until all are finished.

Additional Background Information

Historians who interpreted causes of the Civil War in the years immediately following the conflict wrote from the perspective of firsthand experience and tended to assign guilt to their opponents while justifying the actions of their side. Most historians in the early 1900s presented more complex explanations and stressed that basic institutional and ideological differences made the conflict inevitable. Among these historians were James Ford Rhodes, writing around 1913, and Frank L. Owsley, writing in the early 1930s. In the 1940s "revisionist" historians, including James G. Randall, rejected the notion that the Civil War was inevitable. They blamed the war on irresponsible agitators and blundering statesmen. Still later, historians such as Arthur M. Schlesinger, Jr., rejected the revisionists' view, arguing that a moral evil such as slavery was unlikely to merely fade away and that the potential for compromise was slight. Writing in 1976, David M. Potter argued that the conflict began in the sectional tensions that developed in the 1840s around the Mexican–American War. Today, most historians avoid "blaming" the South for the Civil War and agree that no single explanation can be given for the conflict.

Why the Civil War?
Analyzing One Historian's Interpretation

Writing around 1913 about the causes of the Civil War, historian James Ford Rhodes gives this interpretation.

_____

O f the American Civil War it may safely be asserted that there was a single cause, slavery. . . . [If] the Negro had never been brought to America, our Civil War could not have occurred. . . .

At the time of the formation of the Constitution the two sections were not greatly [different]. A large number of Southern men . . . thought slavery was a moral and political evil to be got rid of gradually . . . [but] invention of the cotton-gin made slavery apparently profitable in the culture of cotton . . . and Southern opinion changed. From being regarded as an evil, slavery began to be looked upon as the only possible condition of the existence of the two races side by side. . . .

In 1831, William Lloyd Garrison began his crusade against slavery. . . . [His] opinion constantly gained ground in the North that slavery was an evil and that its existence was a blot on the national honor. . . .

Through the election of Lincoln the majority of the Northern people declared that slavery was wrong and should not be extended. . . . [The South responded] we can preserve our liberty and our property only by separation.

—From Edwin C. Rozwenc, ed., *The Causes of the American Civil War* (Boston: D.C. Heath, 1961).

Directions

After finishing the reading, give it a title on the title line. Then answer the questions below.

1. If the author had been writing in 1860, what recommendation do you think he would have made about slavery?

_____

_____

_____

2. How do you think the author would assess the abolitionists' role in creating or lessening the tensions that developed between the North and South before the war?

_____

_____

_____

3. Do you think the author would say that the Civil War was inevitable? Explain.

_____

_____

_____

What word or term does the author use to identify the underlying cause of the Civil War?

_____

Why the Civil War?
Analyzing One Historian's Interpretation

Writing in the 1930s about the causes of the Civil War, historian Frank L. Owsley gives this interpretation.

_____

What lay behind the bitter sectional quarreling between 1830 and 1860? What made the war which followed this quarreling so deadly? The answer for these questions and the answer which is yet given by the average Northerner is that the whole struggle from beginning to end was a conflict between light and darkness, between truth and falsehood, between slavery and freedom, between liberty and despotism . . . [but] slavery as a moral issue has too long been [a] red herring [false issue]. . . .

Complex though the factors were which finally caused war, they all grew out of two fundamental differences which existed between the two sections: the North was commercial and industrial, and the South was agrarian. The fundamental and passionate ideal for which the South stood and fell was the ideal of an agrarian society.

This agrarian society had its own interests, which in almost all respects diverged from the interests of the industrial system of the North.

Herein lies the irrepressible conflict, the eternal struggle between the agrarian South and the commercial and industrial North to control the government either in its own interest or, negatively, to prevent the other section from controlling it in its interests.

—From Edwin C. Rozwenc, ed., *The Causes of the American Civil War* (Boston: D.C. Heath, 1961).

Directions

After finishing the reading, give it a title on the title line. Then answer the questions below.

1. If the author had been writing in 1860, what recommendation do you think he would have made about slavery?

_____

_____

_____

2. How would the author assess the abolitionists' role in creating or lessening the tensions that developed between the North and South before the war?

_____

_____

_____

3. Do you think the author would say that the Civil War was inevitable? Explain.

_____

_____

_____

4. What word or term does the author use to identify the underlying cause of the Civil War?

_____

Why the Civil War?
Analyzing One Historian's Interpretation

Writing in the 1940s about the causes of the Civil War, historian James G. Randall gives this interpretation.

_____

War causation tends to be "explained" in terms of great forces. Something elemental is supposed to be at work, be it nationalism, race conflict, or quest for economic advantage. . . . [War seems] in some sense reasonable. . . .

It was small minorities that caused the war; then the regions and sections were drawn in. No one seems to have thought of letting the minorities or the original trouble makers fight it out. . . .

Let one take all the factors [traditionally presented by historians]—the Sumter maneuver, the election of Lincoln, abolitionism, slavery in Kansas, cultural and economic differences—and it will be seen that only by a kind of false display could any of these issues, or all of them together, be said to have caused the war if one omits the elements of emotional unreason and overbold leadership.

If one word or phrase were selected to account for the war, that word would not be slavery, or economic grievance, or state rights, or diverse civilizations. It would have to be such a word as fanaticism (on both sides), misunderstanding, or perhaps politics.

—From Edwin C. Rozwenc, ed., *The Causes of the American Civil War* (Boston: D.C. Heath, 1961).

Directions

After finishing the reading, give it a title on the title line. Then answer the questions below.

1. If the author had been writing in 1860, what recommendation do you think he would have made about slavery?

_____

_____

2. How would the author assess the abolitionists' role in creating or lessening the tensions that developed between the North and South before the war?

_____

_____

3. Do you think the author would say that the Civil War was inevitable? Explain.

_____

_____

4. What word or term does the author use to identify the underlying cause of the Civil War?

_____

Why the Civil War?
Analyzing One Historian's Interpretation

Writing in the 1960s about the causes of the Civil War, historian Arthur M. Schlesinger, Jr., gives this interpretation.

_____

A society closed in the defense of evil institutions . . . creates moral differences far too profound to be solved by compromise. Such a society forces upon every one . . . a moral judgement.

. . . It was the moral issue of slavery, for example, that gave the struggles over slavery in the territories or over enforcement of the fugitive slave laws their significance. These issues . . . were . . . charged with . . . moral and political dynamism. . . .

To say that the Civil War was fought over the "unreal" issue of slavery in the territories is like saying that the Second World War was fought over the "unreal" issue of the invasion of Poland. The democracies could not challenge fascism inside Germany any more than opponents of slavery could challenge slavery inside the South; but the extension of slavery, like the extension of fascism, was an act of aggression which made a moral choice inescapable.

. . . Human slavery is one of the few issues of whose evil we can be sure . . . it is . . . a betrayal of the basic values of our . . . democratic tradition. . . . To reject the moral [character] of the Civil War is to foreclose the possibility of an adequate account of its causes.

—From Edwin C. Rozwenc, ed., *The Causes of the American Civil War* (Boston: D.C. Heath, 1961).

Directions

After finishing the reading, give it a title on the title line. Then answer the questions below.

1. If the author had been writing in 1860, what recommendation do you think he would have made about slavery?

_____

_____

2. How would the author assess the abolitionists' role in creating or lessening the tensions that developed between the North and South before the war?

_____

_____

3. Do you think the author would say that the Civil War was inevitable? Explain.

_____

_____

4. What word or term does the author use to identify the underlying cause of the Civil War?

_____

Why the Civil War?
Analyzing One Historian's Interpretation

Writing in the 1970s about the causes of the Civil War, historian David M. Potter gives this interpretation.

_____

A s the [North and South] became isolated, instead of reacting to each other as they were in actuality, each reacted to a distorted mental image of the other—the North to an image of a southern world of lascivious and sadistic slavedrivers; the South to the image of a northern world of cunning Yankee traders and of rabid abolitionists plotting slave insurrections. This process of substituting stereotypes for realities . . . caused both northerners and southerners to lose sight of how much alike they were and how many values they shared. It also had an effect of changing men's attitudes toward the disagreements which are always certain to arise in politics: ordinary, resolvable disputes were converted into questions of principle, involving rigid, unnegotiable dogma. Abstractions, such as the question of the legal status of slavery in areas where there were no slaves . . . became points of honor and . . . rocked the government to its foundation. . . . Once this divisive tendency set in, sectional rivalry increased the tensions of the slavery issue and the slavery issue embittered sectional rivalries, in a reciprocating process which the majority of Americans found themselves unable to check even though they deplored it.

—From David M. Potter, *The Impending Crisis, 1848–1861* (New York: Harper and Row, 1976).

Directions

After finishing the reading, give it a title on the title line. Then answer the questions below.

1. If the author had been writing in 1860, what recommendation do you think he would have made about slavery?

_____

_____

_____

2. How would the author assess the abolitionists' role in creating or lessening the tensions that developed between the North and South before the war?

_____

_____

_____

3. Do you think the author would say that the Civil War was inevitable? Explain.

_____

_____

_____

4. What word or term does the author use to identify the underlying cause of the Civil War?

_____

About the Activity

In this activity students role play citizen groups advocating five different plans for Reconstruction. In the process, they explore the power struggles over the South's future following the Civil War.

After participating in the activity, students will be able to

- identify unresolved issues at the end of the Civil War.
- describe differences in various groups' goals for Reconstruction.
- take a stand on the most desirable plan for Reconstruction.

Suggested Time: 1 to 2 class periods

Materials: Copies of the goals for five groups, enough of each for one fifth of the class (see the pages following the activity instructions); Activity Sheet 13, one per student

THE ACTIVITY

Getting Started

Begin the activity by asking the class to list some critical problems facing the United States at the conclusion of the Civil War. Responses might include the future of the freedmen, the South's shattered economy, on what terms to readmit the states that had seceded, and how to treat Confederate military and political leaders.

Point out that although the Civil War ended in 1865, many of the attitudes that had led to the war still existed in both North and South. These attitudes made the task of Reconstruction more difficult.

Teaching

Explain to the class that in this activity they will role play representatives of different groups who are appearing before a special committee of the United States Senate to advise on a plan for Reconstruction.

1. Tell students that representatives of five different postwar citizen groups will be appearing before the committee. Identify the groups as Northern Radical Republicans, Northern Moderates, Old Southern Planter Aristocracy and Ex-Confederates, White Small Farmers in the South, and African-American Freedmen.

2. Divide the class into five equal groups and give members of each group a copy of the role description for the citizen group they will represent. Role descriptions are on the pages following these activity instructions. Review the directions and the questions with students.

COMMENTS/NOTES

This activity is most effective when used after students have completed their study of the Civil War but before they have studied Reconstruction.

3. Distribute Activity Sheet 13 to all students and direct them to answer the questions, first individually and then in their groups.

4. When the groups have completed Activity Sheet 13, instruct them to prepare their presentations for the special Senate committee. Their presentations should not only make clear the Reconstruction goals of the citizens they represent but also address the questions raised on Activity Sheet 13. Tell the groups that they are to appoint one or more students to represent their group before the Senate committee.

5. Before beginning the role play, select one student from each of the small groups to serve as a Senate committee member. The students selected should be ones not selected to appear before the committee. Ask the "senators" to sit at the front of the room, then call on groups to make their presentations before the committee in the following order: Northern Radical Republicans, Old Southern Planter Aristocracy and Ex-Confederates, African-American Freedmen, White Small Farmers in the South, and Northern Moderates.

Caution students to listen carefully to the presentations because they will need the information to complete a written assignment at the close of the committee hearing.

After each presentation, allow the senators to ask questions of the presenter or others in that citizen group.

6. When all presentations are completed, allow the senators time to discuss the various presentations and to state their personal views on the merits of each of the goals proposed.

7. At the end of the role play, direct each student to write a letter to the Senate committee proposing a plan for Reconstruction. The plan may be based on the goals of one of the five groups, a combination of several groups' goals, or a completely different set of goals. The letter should begin with a respectful greeting and include a clear statement of position, well-reasoned arguments, and a persuasive style.

Concluding

Conclude the activity by asking students the following questions:

- What issues that contributed to the Civil War remained unsettled at its conclusion?
- Considering the issues and problems that remained after the Civil War, what, if any, purpose do you think the war accomplished?
- What were the strengths and weaknesses of the goals put forth by the five citizen groups represented in the role play?
- What citizens were not represented among the

As students work on Activity Sheet 13, you may wish to stimulate additional thinking by asking the questions provided in the Additional Background Information.

Selecting students from the five groups to represent senators simulates the reality that the senators who made Reconstruction decisions brought varying biases and viewpoints to the task.

Background. A principal question facing the Union was whether the eleven former Confederate states were still part of the Union. Lincoln's position was that the states had never left the Union, but had just been "out of proper relation," and that he, as President, could decide how to set relations right again. Many in Congress, however, contended that the states had seceded and must be readmitted, like new states.

five groups in the role play? (For example, soldiers who fought for the Union were not represented in the groups.)

- Which among the five sets of goals do you think would have led to the "best" Reconstruction plan?

- Are there any problems or tensions remaining in our country today that might stem from the Reconstruction era? If so, how would you characterize them?

Evaluating Student Work

Students may be evaluated on participation in the role play and on their letters, using criteria such as:

- Role play participation should include active contribution during planning, clarity in presenting the group's views (as a presenter), and willingness to answer questions asked by senators.

- Letters should include an appropriate greeting, clear statement of position, two to three supporting arguments, accurate representations of any factual information, and persuasive language.

_____
_____
_____
_____
_____
_____
_____
_____
_____
_____
_____
_____
_____

Additional Background Information

When you discuss the three issues on Activity Sheet 13, asking the following more specific questions may further stimulate student thinking.

Question 1

- Should freed African Americans receive some amount of land from the government?
- Should freed African Americans receive money as compensation for years of unpaid labor? If so, from whom?
- What rights do freed African Americans have under the Constitution?

Question 2

- Should ex-Confederates be able to retain their land?
- Which, if any, ex-Confederates should be singled out for serious punishment?
- What, if any, role should ex-Confederates have in present and future state and local governments?

Question 3

- What role should the Union army play in the South?
- Is the Thirteenth Amendment the only change needed in the Constitution?
- Should the former Confederate states regain the same rights they had under the Constitution before they seceded? Or should the federal government have complete power over them?

Northern Radical Republicans

Directions:

Your job is to assume the role of the group named above. Below is a list of goals your group supports in dealing with post-Civil War problems and issues. Review the goals carefully and use them to complete Activity Sheet 13. Be prepared to present these goals with passion and intensity. They are of vital importance to you!

Goals

- To justify the war by remaking southern society into the image of northern society.
- To punish Confederate leaders politically, but not economically or physically.
- To continue programs such as high tariffs, railroad subsidies, and national banking so economic progress can proceed.
- To keep the Republican party in power.
- To help freedmen make the transition to full freedom by providing them with the vote (suffrage) and economic opportunity.

Northern Moderates

Directions:

Your job is to assume the role of the group named above. Below is a list of goals your group supports in dealing with post-Civil War problems and issues. Review the goals carefully and use them to complete Activity Sheet 13. Be prepared to debate these issues with passion and intensity. They are of vital importance to you!

Goals

- To reconcile the North and South by quickly establishing peace and order.
- To practice leniency, amnesty, and mercy in readmitting the southern states into the Union.
- To maintain capitalist values such as land ownership, free labor, and market competition.
- To let local governments resolve economic and social issues with limited interference by the national government.

Old Southern Planter Aristocracy and Ex-Confederates

Directions:

Your job is to assume the role of the group named above. Below is a list of goals your group supports in dealing with post-Civil War problems and issues. Review the goals carefully and use them to complete Activity Sheet 13. Be prepared to debate these issues with passion and intensity. They are of vital importance to you!

Goals

- To pardon ex-Confederates and return lands that were confiscated by Union forces.
- To restore the South's traditional plantation-based economy by using freed African Americans as a cheap labor force.
- To restore the South's traditional political leaders in the states.
- To restore the traditional social order of the South by giving whites superiority over (but not ownership of) African Americans.

White Small Farmers in the South

Directions:

Your job is to assume the role of the group named above. Below is a list of goals your group supports in dealing with post-Civil War problems and issues. Review the goals carefully and use them to complete Activity Sheet 13. Be prepared to debate these issues with passion and intensity. They are of vital importance to you!

Goals

- To reconcile the North and South by quickly establishing peace and order.
- To recognize the loyalty and economic value of small southern farmers.
- To create greater diversity in the southern economy by investing capital in different types of agriculture.
- To replace the planter aristocracy with new leaders representing other economic interests.
- To limit the powers and rights granted to freedmen and grant suffrage only to the few educated African Americans.

African-American Freedmen

Directions:

Your job is to assume the role of the group named above. Below is a list of goals your group supports in dealing with post-Civil War problems and issues. Review the goals carefully and use them to complete Activity Sheet 13. Be prepared to debate these issues with passion and intensity. They are of vital importance to you!

Goals

- To protect African Americans from abuse and terror by whites.
- To promote economic independence for freedmen by giving them land (40 acres and a mule) and equal opportunity to work in different trades.
- To provide educational opportunities and to restore family and cultural bonds that were broken by the institution of slavery.
- To guarantee equal civil rights and protection under the law.
- To guarantee equal suffrage and political participation for African Americans.

Reconstruction: Whose Plan?
Preparing to Appear before Senators

Directions:

As a group, use your role description and other information from your text to help you answer the questions below. These topics will be part of your Senate testimony and will be debated as a class, so be prepared to defend your positions.

1. What provisions should be made for the freedmen in the South? Are the race issues that, in part, led to the Civil War resolved? Should African Americans have equal rights, including the right to vote?

_____

_____

_____

_____

2. How should the ex-Confederates—who abandoned the Union, pledged their loyalty to the Confederacy, and fought against the Union—now be treated?

_____

_____

_____

_____

3. Who should have greater power in determining the future status of the southern states and the rights of citizens in them: the federal government or each state government?

_____

_____

_____

_____

4. What other important issues, such as the recovery of the southern economy, should be included in Reconstruction plans?

_____

_____

_____

_____

Who Do You Think We Are?
Recognizing Stereotypes

About the Activity

Did stereotyping play a role in the history of western expansion? In this activity students become aware of stereotypes that Native Americans and settlers had of each other.

After participating in the activity, students will be able to

- define and apply the term *stereotype.*
- identify stereotypes that settlers and Native Americans held of each other in the 1800s.
- suggest ways of eliminating stereotypes held by and about present-day individuals and groups.

Planning for the Activity

Suggested Time: 1 class period

Materials: Activity Sheet 14, one per student

THE ACTIVITY

Getting Started

Write the word *stereotype* on the chalkboard and ask students to define it. Write critical elements of their responses on the chalkboard and use the elements to arrive at a definition of stereotype. If necessary, stimulate students' thinking by suggesting the following definitions.

- *a simplified and standardized conception or image invested with special meaning and held in common by members of a group.* (Random House Dictionary of the English Language)
- *a standardized mental picture that is held in common by members of a group and that represents an oversimplified opinion, affective attitude, or uncritical judgment.* (Webster's New Collegiate Dictionary)

Ask the class to identify some perceptions students have of teachers. Write the perceptions on the chalkboard. Then ask the class to identify some perceptions teachers have of students. Post their responses. Apply the definition of stereotype agreed on by the class to the perceptions of students and teachers to determine if the perceptions are stereotypes.

Discuss the origins of the stereotypes. Help students understand that while some perceptions are true for certain individuals or situations, they become stereotypes when inappropriately applied to an entire group of peo-

COMMENTS/NOTES

ple or to all similar situations. Allow volunteers to relate their personal experiences of having been victims of stereotyping.

Teaching

Explain to students that the history of territorial expansion in our nation is replete with examples of stereotypes, held by both Native Americans and settlers. Point out that these stereotypes often led to misunderstanding, distrust, and conflict.

1. Divide the class into small groups of four or five students. Distribute copies of Activity Sheet 14 and explain that students are to brainstorm answers to Questions 1 and 2 on the sheet in their small groups. Suggest that they recall western-era movies and television shows, as well as review information in their texts, for ideas.

2. Review the rules of brainstorming with students and set a time limit of 15 minutes for groups to brainstorm. Instruct each group to appoint an official recorder, but remind students to make individual records of answers to the questions, as well.

3. At the end of 15 minutes, reconvene the class. Collect the answers of the small groups and appoint four students (two for each question) to write the responses on poster paper sheets, so answers can be read from across the room. Emphasize that examples need be posted only once.

4. When the lists are completed, allow time for students to review them individually. Then ask the following questions:

- How would you summarize the stereotypes on the lists?

- Which of the stereotypes can be debunked with factual information? For example, did all Native Americans live in tepees, ride horses, or wear feather headdresses? Did all settlers try to cheat Native Americans in their business dealings?

- How might settlers have acquired their stereotypes of Native Americans?

- How might Native Americans have acquired their view of settlers?

- What role did the superior military strength of the U.S. troops play in forming the stereotypes held by Native Americans and settlers?

- What stereotypes of Native Americans are still held today in this nation? From what sources do those stereotypes come?

Background. An example of the inaccuracies promoted by common stereotypes is the view of Native Americans as "scalping savages." In reality, Native Americans rarely scalped their victims until Europeans began using the scalps of Native Americans as a means of determining bounty. Meanwhile, there were also positive stereotypes of Native Americans. Artists and newspaper reporters were influential in creating images of the "noble savage."

Students may well use racist or insensitive language during brainstorming and debriefing. Emphasize that the use of such language is acceptable in the historical context of the activity but will not be tolerated at any other time in class.

To challenge students' thinking about the origins of Native-American and settler stereotypes, you may wish to read to the class the passage by Patricia Limerick provided in the Additional Background Information, and have students discuss it.

- What stereotypes of settlers are still held today? What sources promote those stereotypes?

Concluding

Ask students to return to their small groups to brainstorm answers to Question 3 on Activity Sheet 14. Instruct groups to be prepared to share their answers. After about 10 minutes in small groups, reconvene the class and review students' examples of present-day stereotyping and their suggestions for eliminating such stereotypes.

Assign students to select from their texts one event involving conflict between settlers and Native Americans and write a one-page essay on how stereotyping by both groups may have contributed to starting or worsening the conflict.

Evaluating Student Work

Students' work may be evaluated on their participation in small and large group discussion as well as the essays.

- Criteria for assessing participation in discussions may include verbal contributions, note-taking, and active listening.
- Criteria for assessing students' essays may include accurate reporting of the conflict, thoughtful identification of possible stereotypes by both parties in the conflict, and logic in drawing conclusions about how the stereotypes may have contributed to the conflict.

_____
_____
_____
_____
_____
_____
_____
_____
_____
_____
_____
_____
_____
_____
_____
_____
_____

Additional Background Information

In her book *The Legacy of Conquest,* historian Patricia Limerick suggests some fundamental differences between Native-American and European-American views and practices, differences that often led to conflicts.

> Euro-American ways of thinking were dominated by the ideas of civilization and savagery. Carrying associations of both nobility and violence, savagery was mankind's childhood, a starting stage in which society drew its shape and order from nature. Savagery meant hunting and gathering, not agriculture; common ownership, not individual property owning; pagan superstition, not Christianity; spoken language, not literacy; emotion, not reason. Savagery had its charms but was fated to yield before the higher stage of civilization represented by white Americans.

The differing perceptions and practices noted by Limerick found their way into the art and literature of the 1800s. The "savagery" of the Native American was frequently juxtaposed with the "civilized nature" of European Americans. The origin of many stereotypes discussed in this activity springs from this perceived distinction.

Who Do You Think We Are?
Identifying Stereotypes

Directions:

In your small group, brainstorm answers to the three questions below.

Question 1: What stereotypes of Native Americans do you think settlers had in the 1800s?

_____

_____

_____

_____

_____

_____

_____

_____

Question 2: What stereotypes of settlers do you think Native Americans had?

_____

_____

_____

_____

_____

_____

_____

_____

Question 3: What stereotypes of racial and ethnic groups exist in our society today? What practical ways can be used to identify and eliminate stereotypes? Be prepared to explain how your ideas could work in specific situations.

_____

_____

_____

_____

_____

_____

_____

_____

Technology: Friend or Foe?
Role Playing Costs and Benefits of Technology

Activity  15

About the Activity

Students role play pro- and anti-technology speakers of the late 1800s, and in the process see how issues surrounding technology more than one hundred years ago continue to confront us today.

After participating in the activity, students will be able to

- identify the costs and benefits of technological development in the United States in the late 1800s.
- compare concerns about technological development in the 1800s with present-day concerns.

Planning for the Activity

Suggested Time: 2–3 class periods

Materials: Activity Sheets 15a and 15b, enough of each for one half of the class; supplies for making graphic materials: poster paper or construction paper, colored markers, scissors, and tape

THE ACTIVITY

Getting Started

Introduce the activity by asking students to identify ten examples of technology that are important in their daily lives. Post their responses on the chalkboard. Ask students to suggest social costs and benefits of each example. Define social costs as disadvantages or harmful effects that are borne by the general public. Define social benefits as advantages or positive effects that accrue to the general public. For example, if the automobile is listed, one of its benefits might be identified as "provides employment for manufacturing workers." One of its costs might be "air pollution."

Have students refer to their texts, or other resources if necessary, to find technological developments in the United States between 1865 and 1910. Examples might include the development of the internal combustion engine, electric motor, storage battery, mechanical looms, refrigeration, standardized parts, and the Bessemer process for making steel. List their examples on the chalkboard. Discuss ways in which these technological developments improved life, as well as the problems they created.

Teaching

Explain to students that they will engage in a role play in which they assume the roles of various people who support and oppose technological development in the late 1800s.

COMMENTS/NOTES

_____

_____

_____

_____

_____

_____

_____

_____

_____

_____

Background. One example of the "costs" of technology during the Industrial Revolution was in the textile industry. Hat makers at that time used mercury for curing felt. Mercury is a deadly poison. Thousands of hat makers suffered from mercury poisoning, developing physical problems as well as a form of insanity known as "hatters' syndrome." From this condition, came the phrase "mad as a hatter."

_____

_____

_____

71

1. Divide students into two equal groups. Assign one group to role play members of the Neo-Luddite group and have them assume specific roles, such as a women's rights activist, a rural craftsperson, a union organizer, a community social worker, and a public health nurse. Distribute to these students Activity Sheet 15a.

Assign the other group to role play members of the Pro-Technocratic Political and Social Club. Instruct students to assume specific roles, such as an inventor of time-saving devices for the home, an economist, a factory owner, and a homemaker. Distribute Activity Sheet 15b to members of this group.

2. Instruct students to read their activity sheet fully, noting the role play instructions at the end of each sheet. Clarify that each group is to make a ten-minute presentation of its point of view on the assigned day. The presentations must include oral statements (speeches), but should also incorporate music, poetry, drama, and/or graphic materials such as posters and handbills. Emphasize that in their presentations students should clearly identify either the main costs or the main benefits of technology.

3. Allow students class time to work on their presentations or assign the preparation as homework.

4. On the day assigned for the role play presentations, explain that each group's ten-minute presentation will be followed by a question-and-answer period. Questions may refer to both the oral presentations and the support materials.

Begin with the Pro-Technocratic group. Direct them to display their support materials and make their presentation. Allow five to ten minutes after the presentations for questions and answers. Follow the same procedure with the Neo-Luddite group.

Concluding

After students' presentations, direct the class in identifying the major social costs and benefits of technological development that were emphasized in the role plays. List these on the chalkboard as they are identified. Ask students to declare whether they would have favored the Neo-Luddites or the Pro-Technocrats had they lived in the late 1800s. Follow up with these questions:

■ In the period of 1865–1910, why was technology often described as a "double-edged sword"? Why is it often described in the same way today?

If necessary, work with both groups of students to develop additional specific roles so that the presentations of the groups will be personal and detailed.

Encourage students to include graphic materials in their presentations, such as political statements and slogans, cartoons, and pictures of important people or events of the period.

Background. In the period 1867–1900, the United States participated in more than a dozen international science and technology expositions. American displays at the exhibitions helped change European attitudes about the quality of American products and created an image of a new and powerful nation.

- Is it desirable, or possible, for the United States to slow the development of technology today?

- Why is technology so attractive today to many people in developing countries?

- Is there a limit to what we can or should do with technological development?

Ask students to summarize what they learned in the activity and to display their graphic materials in the classroom.

Evaluating Student Work

Options for evaluating student work in this activity may include:

- Evaluating students' participation in the planning and development of the role play presentations. Criteria should include initiative, involvement, cooperation, and follow-through.

- Evaluating students' participation in the role-play presentations. Criteria should include overall effort, creativity, use of language, and degree of persuasiveness.

- Evaluating students' participation in the development of graphic materials. Criteria should include creativity, composition, and expression of ideas.

Technology: Friend or Foe?
The Neo-Luddite League

Background

You are a member of the Neo-Luddite League. Your group is named for protestors called Luddites who in 1811 roamed the countryside around Nottingham, England, destroying factory equipment. Historians disagree about the origins of the name "Luddites." A common belief, though, is that the group was named after Ned Ludd, who mentally snapped under the stress of factory work and smashed the equipment on which he was working. His actions resulted in a law being passed to forbid the destruction of industrial equipment. Luddites believed that technology and mechanization had stripped them of their livelihoods as craftsmen and brought unwelcome change and uncertainty to their lives.

As a member of the Neo-Luddite League, you generally believe the following:

- Technology dehumanizes the individual and creates faceless, nameless, one-dimensional human beings.
- Technology destroys traditional values and enslaves people to wasteful consumption.
- Technology destroys human creativity and initiative.

Your Neo-Luddite positions are controversial. Recently, the group has voiced concerns about the situation of factory workers—low wages, long hours, poor and dangerous working conditions, and the relationship of these problems to the conditions of poverty, slum housing, poor sanitation, and disease. You support efforts to unionize workers and believe more government intervention in business and industry is necessary to protect workers and families. With other Luddites, you have attempted to raise citizens' awareness of these problems and to bring about political change.

Your group has supported and seeks support from organizations such as the National Trades Union and various Workingmen's parties. In addition, you support the reform efforts of individuals such as Lucretia Mott and Elizabeth Cady Stanton who champion the rights of women and Catharine Beecher, a leader in the women's education movement.

The Situation

Today you and other members of the League are meeting to prepare a peaceful protest at a public exhibition showcasing new technological developments. You expect to make speeches, give presentations, display posters, and distribute handbills to promote your beliefs. Your group's presentation should include a clear statement of the costs of technological development. Such costs might include loss of cottage industry jobs and abuse of factory workers.

In the time provided, you are to work with other Neo-Luddites to organize and develop your strategies and materials and to choose roles for the role play.

Technology: Friend or Foe?
The Pro-Technocratic Political and Social Club

Background

You are a member of the Pro-Technocratic Political and Social Club. Your group was formed to support the belief that technological development is good for society. The purpose of the club is to promote technological innovation through political and social means.

As a member of the club, you generally believe the following:

- Technology brings personal freedom from constraints imposed on human beings by nature, tradition, and rigid social patterns.
- Technology releases women and children from the ancient bonds of marital and parental authority by providing them employment opportunities.
- Technology is the means by which a society achieves stability, growth, and prestige.
- Technology frees people from hard physical labor.

When asked to describe how technology helps society, your group often notes that the technology-rich textile industry has helped create better quality and a wider selection of cloth products at lower prices. As a result, consumers can purchase a greater variety of warmer, more durable clothing. Pro-Technocrats also argue that the textile industry helps society by employing many workers, who stimulate local economies and the national economy by spending or saving their earnings.

You list the following individuals and their accomplishments as among the people you most admire: Eli Whitney—interchangeable parts and mass production, Elias Howe—sewing machine, Charles Goodyear—vulcanized rubber, Samuel F. B. Morse—telegraph, John Deere—steel plow, and Cyrus McCormick—the mechanical reaper.

The Situation

Today, you and other club members are meeting to prepare a presentation at a public exhibition that will showcase new technological innovations and production processes. Your main purpose is to call attention to the social and economic benefits of new technology. You also intend to warn against efforts by union organizers, government, and Neo-Luddites to limit the freedom of business leaders and industrialists to develop and expand technology. You expect to make speeches, give presentations, display posters, and distribute handbills to promote your beliefs. Include in your group's presentation a clear statement of the benefits of technological development and growth, industrialization, and big business.

In the time provided, you should work with other Pro-Technocratic club members to organize and develop strategies and materials and to choose roles for the role play.

"Dear Captain of Industry"
Exchanging Letters Between Industrialists and Workers

 *Activity* **16**

About the Activity

Playing the roles of industrialists and workers in the late 1800s and early 1900s, students write letters to each other expressing differing viewpoints on the impact of industry.

After participating in the activity, students will be able to

- describe beliefs, values, and lifestyles of industrialists in the late 1800s and early 1900s.
- describe the beliefs, values, and lifestyles of factory workers in the late 1800s and early 1900s.
- identify advantages and disadvantages of industrial growth.

Planning for the Activity

Suggested Time: 2 class periods

Materials: Activity Sheets 16a and 16b, one of each per student

Advance Preparation: In this activity students are required to do research. To direct their efforts, you may wish to suggest or bring to class resources with information on the following topics: the growth of such industries as oil, steel, and railroads; major figures such as John D. Rockefeller, Andrew Carnegie, and Henry Clay Frick; the creation and perpetuation of trusts; conditions of the working class; philosophical ideas such as Social Darwinism and laissez-faire capitalism; conditions of city life faced by urban workers, especially newly arriving immigrants.

THE ACTIVITY

Getting Started

Ask students to name contemporary Americans they think of as wealthy. Identify the sources of these people's wealth. Call on students to identify the family names in American history they most associate with wealth. Continue the discussion until students have named Rockefeller, and perhaps Carnegie or Frick. Probe to see if they know the source of the Rockefeller wealth and the time period in which the Rockefeller family first came into prominence.

Teaching

Explain to the class that in this activity they will compare how the growth of industry affected both industrialists and industrial workers in the late 1800s and early 1900s.

1. Assign one half of the class to play the role of industrialists, or "captains of industry." Tell the other half that they will play the role of average workers.

2. Distribute Activity Sheet 16a. Review the directions and questions with students. They are to complete only the questions for the role they have been assigned. Direct

COMMENTS/NOTES

This activity is designed as a conclusion to a unit of study on industrialism in the late 1800s and early 1900s.

_____

_____

_____

_____

_____

_____

_____

_____

_____

To facilitate students' research, you might wish to gather some resources from the library and make them available in your classroom. You may also assign research as homework.

77

students to gather information from their texts or other supplemental materials.

3. After students have done their research, have the "industrialists" gather on one side of the classroom and the "workers" on the other. Divide each large group into groups of four or five students. Distribute copies of Activity Sheet 16b to all students.

4. Tell the class that each small group will have 10 minutes to pool their research information in order to help each other complete Activity Sheet 16b. Emphasize that they should clearly and concisely identify their positions and opinions.

5. After the 10 minutes of group work, direct students to form pairs, with each pair consisting of an industrialist and a worker. When partners are identified, have students return to their industrialist or worker locations and be seated.

6. Explain to the workers that they will have 10 minutes to write letters to their partners, the captains of industry, to describe how their working conditions affect their lives. In their letters, the workers are also to ask for an explanation of why industry does not reward its workers more generously and provide better working conditions for them. As the workers write, direct the industrialists to prepare to respond by anticipating what the workers will write.

7. After 10 minutes, direct the workers to give their letters to their industrialist partners. Instruct the industrialists to read the letters and respond in letters explaining how, from their perspective, the American economy works, their role in it, and why the practices they follow are important to the growth of the nation. Industrialists should make clear to the workers that life for those who "drive the engine of progress" is also difficult. Industrialists' letters should be written in a style appropriate to a captain of industry. Tell the industrialists they have 12 minutes to complete their task. As the industrialists write, workers should prepare to respond by anticipating what the industrialists will write.

8. After 12 minutes, have the industrialists present their letters to the workers. Explain that the workers have 7 minutes to read the letters and respond with second letters in which they identify five practices or premises of industry they believe must change. They are to explain why each reform is needed.

9. After 7 minutes, direct workers to give their second letters to their industrialist partners. Instruct the industrialists to read the letters and then respond, describing the five aspects of industry of which they are most proud. Allow 7 minutes for this task.

Background. Among the resources you might call to students' attention are Upton Sinclair's *The Jungle,* William O'Neill's *Women at Work* (Quadrangle Press), and Rebecca Harding Davis's *Life in the Iron Mills* (The Feminist Press).

78

10. End the letter rotation by having the workers read the industrialists' second letters.

Concluding

Collect the four letters from each pair, and then ask students to consider their letters as they answer the following questions.

- What were the basic concerns and premises of the workers?
- What were the basic concerns and premises of the industrialists?
- What aspects of industry created the most pride among industrialists?
- What practices did workers feel most needed change?
- Based on your study of this era, do you think industrialists are best described as "Captains of Industry" or "Robber Barons"? Explain.
- What is your personal reaction to the conditions of labor at that time in history?

Evaluating Student Work

Letters written by students may be used to evaluate their understanding. Criteria may include the following:

- Worker letters: detailed descriptions of dangerous and unsanitary conditions, long hours, child labor, corrupt payment and loan schemes, paid informers, and the dulling effect of factory organization. Letters should demand that industrialists answer questions such as why workers receive so little reward for their work and are subjected to inhumane conditions.

- Industrialist letters: written with an imperious tone and communicating the belief that as captains of industry, industrialists have provided many jobs for workers. The letters should suggest that if workers have not bettered themselves it is because they have not taken advantage of the economic opportunities available in the United States. These letters should also emphasize the contributions made by industrialists to the economic well being of the entire society, contributions that include both the financing of industrial growth and charitable donations (hospitals, museums, symphonies, etc.).

Background. The theory of Social Darwinism held that the wealthy were those who had risen to the top in a struggle for profits that rewarded the strong and eliminated the weak. It also held that slum conditions were natural for the unfit who, by lack of thrift and industriousness, had lost in the economic struggle.

Additional Background Information

Although most workers in this period labored under difficult, often inhumane, working conditions, many took actions to prevent themselves from being totally victimized. One example of such action was the formation of ethnic communities in which workers cared for the families of other workers who were killed or disabled. For example, a disabled Irish miner might be set up in a new business with funds collected from other Irish miners. The contributing miners owned the business, and the disabled worker was its lifetime manager. Some communities even supported a local agent to help unemployed workers find other jobs or to negotiate disputes with industry owners. In some respects these self-help practices were the forerunners of labor unions.

"Dear Captain of Industry"
Researching Information on Industrialists and Workers

Directions:

Your task is to research your assigned role as either an industrialist or a worker during the late 1800s and early 1900s. Use the questions on this sheet to help organize your research. You will need the information you collect for other tasks in the activity. On the first line, identify yourself as an industrialist or a worker.

Role _____

1. Describe your daily life. List as many specific details of your work and personal life as possible.

_____
_____
_____
_____
_____
_____

2. Describe your philosophy of life and work. Identify your personal goals and your beliefs about your responsibilities to society.

_____
_____
_____
_____
_____
_____

3. List other details you discover through research about either the life of workers or the life of industrialists. For example, how did industrialists acquire their wealth and what did they do with their money? Who were the workers and what were their experiences before becoming industrial workers?

_____
_____
_____
_____
_____

"Dear Captain of Industry"
Sharing Research Information

Directions:

Working with members of your group, complete the tasks below. Share the information you collected on Activity Sheet 16a and take notes on information provided by others in your group. Make good use of your sharing time because you will need the information to complete the next phase of the activity.

1. List facts, ideas, and opinions that are important in describing and persuasively stating your position as a worker or an industrialist.

_____

_____

_____

_____

_____

_____

_____

2. Identify the key values underlying your position and opinions. In other words, what are your basic beliefs?

_____

_____

_____

_____

_____

_____

3. Identify and list the viewpoints you believe people in the other role hold. Develop arguments against their views.

_____

_____

_____

_____

_____

_____

_____

About the Activity

In cooperative learning groups, students teach each other the basic goals of the Progressive party, using the party's platform of 1912. Then they create cartoons illustrating progressive beliefs. Finally, they explore the question "What did the Progressives ever do for you?"

After participating in the activity, students will be able to

- identify and explain specific beliefs and goals of the Progressive party.
- describe the impact of Progressive-era reforms on present-day Americans.

Planning for the Activity

Suggested Time: 1 to 2 class periods

Materials: Activity Sheets 17a through 17c, one copy of each per student

THE ACTIVITY

Getting Started

Challenge students to recall what they may have previously read or heard about the Progressive party or the progressive movement. Post their responses on the chalkboard. Allow the class to confirm or refute the posted information by using their texts or other classroom resources.

If students are unfamiliar with the Progressive party, explain briefly that it was part of an important political movement in the early 1900s. Among its other goals, the Progressive party sought to elect state and federal officials who would improve the conditions of the poor and working classes.

Teaching

Explain to the class that the Progressive party's beliefs and its goals were best expressed in the party's 1912 platform.

1. Distribute copies of Activity Sheets 17a through 17c and explain that they provide excerpts from the 1912 Progressive party platform. Clarify the directions with students, emphasizing that while they will analyze and interpret their assigned section of the platform with others in a small group, they will each be responsible for teaching about the section to students who have not studied it.

2. Before dividing the class into groups, direct students' attention to the platform's introduction. Ask them to read and make notes on their interpretation of it.

COMMENTS/NOTES

Background. The Progressive party grew out of a split in the Republican party when Republican leaders ruled against Theodore Roosevelt's delegates at their 1912 national convention. Roosevelt's followers drafted the Progressive party platform at the Progressive party convention in Chicago on August 3, 1912. The progressive movement was wider than the party itself.

Background. The Progressive party platform casts its goals in terms of justice and a government "of the people, by the people, and for the people." By stating goals in this

3. Divide the class into four equal groups. Assign each group one of the four sections (A, B, C, D) into which the platform is divided on the activity sheets. Instruct the groups to develop their interpretations and explanations of their assigned sections in an allotted time, 10 to 15 minutes. Emphasize that they are to become "experts" on their section.

4. At the end of the allotted time, organize students into "teaching groups." Every teaching group should consist of four students, each an expert on a different section of the platform. The task is for each student to teach the other members of the group about his or her section. When teaching, students should focus on the beliefs, goals, and specific program proposals set forth in the platform. When not teaching, students should take notes and ask clarifying questions so that they have a clear understanding of the entire platform.

5. After the teaching groups are finished, conduct a class discussion of the beliefs, goals, and program proposals of the Progressive party by asking the following questions:

- How would you characterize the beliefs of the Progressive party? Who were the party's enemies? Which groups of citizens did the party want to attract to party membership or to support progressive causes?

- What party goals are outlined in the Progressives' platform? With which of these goals do you agree or disagree?

- How do the Progressive party's goals relate to events in United States history in the late 1800s and early 1900s? In particular, is there a relationship between the Progressive party and the growth of industrialization?

- What proposals of the progressives are part of our present-day lives?

- What legacies or accomplishments of the progressive movement would you judge most important?

Concluding

Direct students to review the Progressive party platform and then draw an editorial cartoon to illustrate one or more of the party's beliefs, goals, or program proposals. For example, a cartoon might depict the corruptness of the "old" parties by showing a politician giving a speech praising big business for its donations to charities while a hand representing big business is shoving money into the politician's back pocket.

language, the party implied that the government had been taken away from the "people."

Make dictionaries available to students, clarifying that they are responsible for learning definitions of words with which they are unfamiliar.

If there are not enough students to create groups of four, two or three students may work together and call on other students for help as needed.

Evaluating Student Work

Students' work may be evaluated on their small group teaching and their cartoons.

- Criteria for evaluating small group teaching may include evidence of understanding, clarity in presenting information, and skill in responding to questions.
- Criteria for evaluating cartoons may include the cartoon's clarity, creativity, and relevance to the Progressive platform.

While students should not be graded on their artistic ability, it is important to acknowledge such talent in the completed cartoons.

Additional Background Information

The work of the progressive movement resulted in a number of significant reforms that affect our lives today. Progressives were responsible for beginning federal regulation and oversight of food and drugs by marshalling passage of the Pure Food and Drug Act. They also helped bring about new safety regulations in industry, improvement in the working conditions of children and women, and the eight-hour workday. Political reforms that are linked to the Progressive party include the direct election of federal senators and the institution of recall, referendum, and initiative at local and state levels. Progressives were also successful in promoting anti-trust legislation that ultimately placed some limitations on big business.

Some Progressive Thinking
Interpreting the 1912 Progressive Party Platform

Directions:

On the left side of this sheet are excerpts from the Progressive party platform of 1912. With members of your group, read and interpret your assigned section of the platform. Focus on identifying the Progressive party's **beliefs, goals,** and **program proposals.** When you are familiar with your section of the platform, you will teach others about it. Use the right-hand column for taking notes to use in your presentation and to summarize what you learn about the other sections.

The Progressive Party Platform

Introduction The conscience of the people, in a time of grave national problems, has called into being a new party, born of the nation's sense of justice. We of the Progressive Party here dedicate ourselves to the fulfillment of the duty laid upon us by our fathers to maintain the government of the people, by the people, and for the people whose foundations they laid. . . .

A. The Old Parties Political Parties exist to secure responsible government and to execute the will of the people.

From these great tasks both of the old parties have turned aside. . . . They have become the tools of corrupt interests which use them impartially to serve their selfish purposes. . . . To dissolve the unholy alliance between corrupt business and corrupt politics is the first task. . . . [Our] new party offers itself as the instrument of the people to sweep away old abuses, to build a new and nobler commonwealth. . . .

The Rule of the People . . . In particular, the party declares for direct primaries for the nomination of State and National officers, for nation-wide preferential primaries for candidates for the presidency; for the direct election of United States senators by the people; and we urge on the States the policy of the short ballot, with responsibility to the people secured by the initiative, referendum and recall. . . .

My Interpretation

Some Progressive Thinking
Interpreting the 1912 Progressive Party Platform

Equal Suffrage The Progressive Party, believing that no people can justly claim to be a true democracy which denies political rights on account of sex, pledges itself to the task of securing equal suffrage to men and women alike.

B. Corrupt Practices We pledge our party to legislation that will compel strict limitation of all campaign contributions and expenditures, and detailed publicity of both before as well as after primaries and elections.

Publicity and Public Service We pledge our party to legislation compelling the registration of lobbyists; publicity of committee hearings except on foreign affairs, and recording of all votes in committee. . . .

Administration of Justice . . . We believe . . . that a person cited for contempt in labor disputes, except when such contempt was committed in the actual presence of the court . . . should have a right to trial by jury.

C. Social and Industrial Justice The supreme duty of the Nation is the conservation of human resources through social and industrial justice. We pledge ourselves to work unceasingly in State and Nation for:

Effective legislation looking to the prevention of industrial accidents, occupational diseases, overwork, involuntary unemployment, and other injurious effects incident to modern industry;

The fixing of minimum safety and health standards for the various occupations . . . and the public authority of State and Nation . . . to maintain such standards;

Some Progressive Thinking
Interpreting the 1912 Progressive Party Platform

The prohibition of child labor;

Minimum wage standards for working women . . . ;

The general prohibition of night work for women and the establishment of an eight-hour day for women and young persons;

One day's rest in seven for all wage workers;

. . . Standards of compensation for death by industrial accident and injury and trade diseases which will transfer the burden of lost earnings from the families of working people to the industry, and thus to the community;

The protection of home life against the hazards of sickness, irregular employment, and old age through the adoption of a system of social insurance. . . .

We favor the organization [into unions] of the workers, men and women, as a means of protecting their interests and promoting their progress. . . .

D. Conservation . . . We believe that the remaining forests, coal and oil lands, water powers, and other natural resources still in State or National control (except agricultural lands) are more likely to be wisely conserved and utilized for the general welfare if held in the public hands.

In order that consumers and producers, managers and workmen, now and hereafter, need not pay toll to private monopolies of power and raw material, we demand that such resources shall be retained by the State or Nation, and opened to immediate use under laws which will encourage development and make to the people a moderate return for benefits conferred. . . .

Yellow Journalism and You
Writing News Accounts of the *Maine* Sinking

Activity **18**

About the Activity

In this activity, students write and compare accounts of the sinking of the U.S.S. *Maine* from six different points of view. In the process they gain insights into the nature of the emotional reporting known as yellow journalism.

After participation in the activity, students will be able to

- describe the journalistic style known as yellow journalism.
- recognize how news accounts can promote a particular point of view.

Planning for the Activity

Suggested Time: 2 class periods

Materials: Activity Sheets 18a and 18b, one of each per student

THE ACTIVITY

Getting Started

Introduce the activity by writing the term *yellow journalism* on the chalkboard and asking students to write a definition or short explanation of it. Call on volunteers to share their definitions. If students have not previously encountered the term, refer them to their text, dictionaries, or other references.

Discuss different functions of the press, such as providing objective news, promoting particular points of view, and making a profit by building readership and advertising revenues. Then ask students how these functions might conflict with each other and why they think journalists might engage in yellow journalism.

Teaching

Explain that in this activity students will first read an account of the sinking of the U.S.S. *Maine* in Havana harbor on February 15, 1898. Remind the class that this was a precipitating factor in the Spanish-American War. Tell students that after reading the account, they will write a news report from one of several perspectives.

1. Provide each student with a copy of Activity Sheet 18a. After they have read the account, discuss the following questions:

- What was the relationship between Spain and Cuba in 1898?

COMMENTS/NOTES

_____

_____

_____

_____

_____

_____

_____

_____

_____

_____

_____

Background. Perhaps at no time has American public opinion been more influenced by newspaper journalism than during the Cuban Revolution and Spanish-American War. Although most American newspapers favored United States intervention in the Cuban conflict, the emotional coverage of William Randolph Hearst's New York *Journal* and Joseph Pulitzer's *World* was especially influential. Some historians say that the Cuban revolution was just convenient ammunition for the circulation war between the two newspapers.

Explain to students that the historical account on Activity Sheet 18a is a compilation of facts from several sources

- Why were Cubans rebelling against Spain?

- Why were some people in the United States interested in Cuba?

- What was President McKinley's position on the Cuban Revolution?

2. Provide each student with a copy of Activity Sheet 18b. Divide the class into six groups and assign a different reporter role to each group.

3. Explain that each student is to write a news report describing the sinking of the *Maine* from the perspective of his or her assigned reporter. Students should consider their purpose and intended audience. Allow time for them to talk with other members of their group about the approach their reporter might take.

4. Read aloud one report for each role, without identifying roles. Have students hypothesize about each role and explain their hypothesis.

Concluding

Have authors of the articles you read aloud identify their roles. Then discuss the following questions:

- How did the Socha report differ from the rest?

- In what ways were the Berra and Smith reports different from the others?

- Which reports were most representative of yellow journalism? Based on these reports, how would you characterize yellow journalism?

- In what ways do individual journalists and the press in general influence the public? Should newspapers attempt to influence the public to adopt a particular point of view?

- What examples of yellow journalism do you see in today's news media?

Call on volunteers to summarize what they learned.

Evaluating Student Work

Options for evaluating student work include:

- assessing individual participation in the large and small group discussions. Criteria might include co-operation, accuracy and clarity of answers to questions, and effective listening.

- assessing news reports. Criteria might include understanding the perspective, creativity, persuasiveness, and appropriate language.

and that it attempts to be objective. Ask students to consider whether any account can be truly unbiased.

_____

_____

_____

_____

Before students write their accounts, have them refer to the information in their texts and other reference books on the Cuban revolution, the sinking of the U.S.S. *Maine*, and the Spanish-American War.

_____

_____

_____

_____

_____

_____

_____

_____

_____

_____

_____

_____

_____

_____

_____

_____

_____

_____

_____

Yellow Journalism and You
Reading an Historical Account of the *Maine* Sinking

At approximately 9:40 p.m. on February 15, 1898, the U.S.S. *Maine* exploded and sank in Havana harbor. At least 200 seamen were reported missing and presumed dead as a result of the tragedy. A crew of 320 was on board the ship at the time of the explosion. Of 26 officers, 22 were on the ship. The American steamer *City of Washington* was also in the harbor, but no damage was reported to it.

The cause of the disaster was undetermined. Possible explanations included a bomb or a torpedo, an explosion in the weapons storage area, carelessness, or natural causes.

The U.S.S. *Maine* had been ordered to Havana on January 24, 1898, to protect United States citizens living on the island. Several weeks earlier, riots in Havana were thought to be endangering them and their property. Later, the Havana riots were determined to have been led by Spanish soldiers, who apparently objected to articles published in four Cuban newspapers about the Spanish army and its officers. The riots were directed against the newspaper offices, not American citizens. No American was proved to have been hurt or endangered during the riots.

Since 1895 Cuban revolutionaries had sought Cuban independence from Spain. The American people had generally sided with the revolutionaries in the dispute. Sympathy and support for the Cuban people had been publicly expressed by many groups, including the Socialist Labor Party, the Knights of Labor, and the American Federation of Labor.

The sinking of the *Maine* provided Americans with the opportunity to consider intervention in foreign affairs. In the case of the conflict between Cuba and Spain, few United States citizens seemed to object to intervention. Some argued that intervention was necessary because the United States must always come to the defense of the "underdog." Others suggested that, like the American colonies in 1776, every territory deserves to be free of its mother country. Many others supported intervention to protect American business and economic interests in Cuban sugar and tobacco.

Unlike former President Grover Cleveland, who proclaimed American neutrality in the conflict between Cuba and Spain, President McKinley had expressed approval of popular support for the Cuban revolutionaries. However, upon hearing about the sinking of the *Maine*, McKinley asked the nation to withhold judgment until the official inquiry could be completed.

Yellow Journalism and You
Identifying Reporter Roles

Role 1   Pedro Campos, Cuban journalist with the Cuban-American newspaper *Patria*. Mr. Campos and the newspaper are strong supporters of the Cuban revolutionary movement. Patria is produced and distributed in the United States and provides daily reports to other American newspapers. Campos is on assignment in Havana.

Role 2   Federico Perez, Spanish journalist with the Spanish newspaper *El Heraldo de Madrid*. Mr. Perez has been assigned to Cuba to report on the Cuban revolution. His articles are influential among Spanish government officials. Both he and the newspaper are opposed to the Cuban revolution.

Role 3   Harold McNoyton, American journalist for the United States newspaper *Business in Perspective*. Mr. McNoyton has been assigned to Cuba to report the effects of the revolution on United States business interests. He is considered the top business analyst in the United States. He is also rumored to have investments in the Cuban tobacco industry.

Role 4   Frederick Socha, press aide to President McKinley assigned to Cuba to follow and report on the revolution. Each day Mr. Socha prepares and sends a telegram to the President's press secretary. The telegrams are intended to inform the President of daily events in Cuba.

Role 5   Sonny Berra, American reporter for the New York *World*. The *World* strongly supports United States intervention in Cuba. On January 24, 1898, after learning that the U.S.S. *Maine* had been sent to Cuba, the *World* featured an editorial titled, "Our Flag in Havana at Last." The *World* is involved in a newspaper war with its major competitor, the New York *Journal*. The *World* was one of the first newspapers to use yellow journalism.

Role 6   Albert Smith, American reporter with the New York *Journal*. The *Journal* strongly supports the Cuban revolution against Spain. It is in a newspaper war with the New York *World*. The *Journal* has been accused of creating stories and sensationalizing events in Cuba to gain readers. The *Journal* is one of the newspapers responsible for initiating yellow journalism.

About the Activity

Where should the government draw the line on liberty? In this activity students learn that the issue of weighing individual liberties against national security, first debated in 1798, once again emerged in World War I. Taking stands on three cases, students participate in a fishbowl discussion.

After participating in the activity, students will be able to

- describe the intent of the Espionage and Sedition Acts of 1917–1918.
- defend or oppose the suppression of civil liberties in wartime.

Planning for the Activity

Suggested Time: 1 to 2 class periods

Materials: Activity Sheet 19, one copy per student

Advance Preparation: This activity will be most effective after students have studied the events leading up to the United States' entry into World War I.

THE ACTIVITY

Getting Started

Introduce the activity by asking students to identify rights protected by the First Amendment. List them on the chalkboard. Then ask under what circumstances, if any, they think the freedoms of speech, press, and assembly should be limited. (Students may note situations involving threats to public safety, such as yelling "fire" in a crowded theater; libel or slander; actions seen as a threat to public morality, such as pornography sold in bookstores; and actions seen as threats to national security, such as war protesters blocking the entrance to a military recruitment center.) Probe for students' reasons for and against limitations.

Teaching

Explain that some of the most vigorous debates over limiting freedom of speech, press, and assembly have focused on situations affecting national security. Tell students that the issue arose again before and during World War I.

1. Ask students to note a time before 1900 in which First Amendment rights were limited in the name of protecting national security. If they do not recall the Sedition Act of 1798, refer them to their text or to Activity Sheet 7a. Discuss the principles and specific cases arising from the Sedition Act and emphasize that it was later repealed.

COMMENTS/NOTES

Background. The First Amendment guarantees freedom of religion, speech, free press, peaceful assembly, and petition.

Note examples of First Amendment cases being reported in your local press.

2. Review with students the events and climate of opinion leading up to World War I and the United States' entry into it. Then share the Additional Background Information on the Espionage Act of 1917 and the Sedition Act of 1918 (see page 96).

3. Distribute copies of Activity Sheet 19. Instruct students to read about the cases and prepare an argument for or against the government actions in each case.

4. Have students move their desks into a large circle. Inside the large circle arrange six desks or chairs in a smaller circle, referred to as the "fishbowl." Tell students that six of them will be selected to sit in the fishbowl and present their arguments for or against the government actions taken in the cases on Activity Sheet 19.

Only students seated in the fishbowl will be allowed to speak. However, those in the outside circle who wish to speak may move to the inner circle and stand behind a student who has already spoken. Students in the fishbowl are required to give their seats to persons standing behind them and to move to a vacant desk in the outer circle. Point out that students will be evaluated on the amount and quality of their participation.

5. Identify six students who are willing to discuss Case 1: three who support the government's action and three who oppose it. Have them move to the six fishbowl chairs. Call on one student to present his or her argument. Continue until all six volunteers have presented, and any outer-circle students who wish to participate have moved into the fishbowl and spoken.

6. Continue in the same manner with cases 2 and 3, beginning each discussion with six volunteers in the fishbowl circle.

Concluding

After the fishbowl discussions, ask the following questions of the whole class:

- Is national security a concern serious enough to warrant restricting First Amendment rights?

- What criteria should be used to determine if a particular action by an individual or group is a serious enough threat to national security to warrant restricting First Amendment rights? For example, do lives need to be endangered or is a threat to public morale sufficient cause?

- Does the ability of the federal government to restrict constitutionally guaranteed rights provide greater or lesser security to citizens?

- Why might some people argue strongly against any suppression of citizen rights?

To conclude, assign students to write a one-page essay entitled "Individual Rights vs. National Security." Students

Background. In the 1919 case *Schenck* v. *U.S.,* the Supreme Court upheld a conviction under the Espionage Act. In declaring the Court opinion Justice Oliver Wendell Holmes wrote, "Words can be weapons. . . . The question in every case is whether the words used are used in such circumstances and are of such a nature as to create a clear and present danger." This statement became known as the "clear and present danger" doctrine.

If the classroom does not lend itself to the fishbowl arrangement, you may position the six chairs in a row at the front of the room.

_____

_____

_____

_____

_____

_____

_____

_____

_____

_____

_____

_____

_____

_____

Background. In 1940 the Smith Act, a response to the growing threat of world war, reinforced the Espionage and Sedition Acts of 1917–1918. Since the passage of the Smith Act, the Supreme Court has more narrowly defined the circumstances under which people can be convicted of endangering national security.

_____

_____

_____

_____

_____

should discuss both the 1798 and 1918 Sedition Acts, and then support their opinions on whether there is likely to be more or less government restriction of rights in the future.

Evaluating Student Work

Options for assessing student work include:

- evaluating on the fishbowl participation on the basis of number of contributions, understanding of historical facts and principles, logic, persuasiveness, and use of concrete examples to support their arguments.

- evaluating essays on the basis of clarity in assessing similarities and differences between the 1798 and 1918 Sedition Acts and persuasive use of supporting examples.

Additional Background Information

In 1917 Congress passed the Espionage Act. Consisting of a number of bills prepared by the Attorney General, this legislation provided for a fine of $10,000 and up to twenty years in prison for any person who, during wartime, was found guilty of willfully making false statements with the intent of interfering with the war effort; promoting the success of the enemy; causing insubordination, disloyalty, mutiny, or refusal of duty in the armed forces; or interfering with armed forces recruitment. An additional provision of the act directed post office officials to exclude any material deemed to violate the act or to provoke or urge treason, insurrection, or resistance to any federal law. The Sedition Act, passed in 1918, extended the power of the United States government over speech and printed opinion. The act prohibited disloyal, profane, or abusive remarks about the form of government, flag, or military uniforms of the United States, and any language intended to obstruct the war effort in any way. The Postmaster General was empowered to deny the use of the mail to any person who, in his or her opinion, used the mails to violate the act. The Sedition Act outlawed nearly all criticism of the war and the government.

Both the Sedition Act of 1798 and the Sedition Act of 1918 were designed to protect the United States from "internal" enemies in a time of crisis. However, both acts also raised the issue of the balance between citizen rights and national security. In 1798 the Federalists argued that strong power and authority were the means to ensure political stability and security and to avoid tyranny. The Republicans countered with the argument that security could only be assured through personal liberty and a government reflecting the will of the people. Republicans thought the proposed Alien and Sedition Acts violated the First Amendment and would result in tyranny. Nevertheless, the Federalist-controlled Congress passed both acts. During World War I the Wilson administration sought security and stability through broad power and authority under the Espionage and Sedition Acts of 1917 and 1918.

Rights in Wartime: World War I
Taking a Stand on Charges of Sedition

Directions:

The following cases describe government actions taken against United States citizens during World War I. Read each case and prepare an argument to support or oppose the government's action.

Case 1

In a speech to a small crowd in 1917, Kate Richards O'Hare told mothers they were no better than breeding pigs if they let the government send their sons to Europe to fight and die. As a result of the speech, Mrs. O'Hare was arrested and charged with violating the Espionage Act by obstructing enlistment. She was found guilty and sentenced to five years in a federal penitentiary.

Case 2

On June 16, 1917, Postmaster General Albert S. Burleson directed local postmasters to watch for newspapers and magazines containing materials that might cause insubordination, disloyalty, mutiny, or other actions that might obstruct the government's war effort. Within a month of Burleson's declaration, many publications had been excluded from the mail, including the magazine *Masses. Masses* sought readers among young intellectuals and took a strong stand against the war in its articles and cartoons. Convicted under the Espionage Act, the publishers of *Masses* had their second-class mailing privileges revoked.

Case 3

After 1918, some 2,100 persons were indicted under the provisions of the Sedition Act. Among them was Walter Matthey of Iowa. Matthey attended a meeting where, according to the Iowa Attorney General, he listened to a speech in which disloyal statements were made, applauded some of the statements, and contributed 25 cents to the meeting's organizers. Matthey was later arrested, charged with violating the Sedition Act, and sentenced to one year in jail.

All the News That's Fit to Print
Creating a Newspaper on the 1920s

Activity 20

About the Activity

To capture the excitement and tensions of the 1920s, students work in groups to create newspapers reflecting events and life during the Twenties.

After participating in the activity, students will be able to

- identify significant events, people, values, and themes from the 1920s.
- describe major topics of the 1920s by writing in various journalistic formats.

Planning for the Activity

Suggested Time: 2 or more class periods; out-of-class research and writing

Materials: Activity Sheet 20, one per student; copies of two or more current newspapers by different publishers; poster paper; glue; tape; scissors; markers

Advance Preparation: This activity is most effective when completed over a one-week period, with students doing work in and out of class. A suggested schedule is as follows: Monday—introduce project, form small groups, make individual assignments; Tuesday—provide in-class research time; Wednesday—assign out-of-class research and writing tasks; Thursday—provide some in-class time for peer review and editing of articles and planning for final newspaper assembly; Friday—devote period to in-class assembly of newspapers, review, and debriefing.

THE ACTIVITY

Getting Started

Ask students to describe the newspaper format, noting division into sections, use of headlines and bylines, and integration of graphics (pictures, charts, graphs) with text. Have them study the newspapers you have brought to class, noting similarities and differences.

Teaching

Explain that in this activity students will work in groups to create a newspaper about the 1920s. Their papers are to inform the reader about life throughout the 1920s decade, not just one day or year.

1. Divide the class into small groups of five students and clarify that each group will create a newspaper.

2. Distribute Activity Sheet 20 and review the directions. Specify the date on which the newspapers will be due and interim project deadlines.

3. Set aside time during one class period before the project due date for group members to exchange articles and pictures for critiquing and proofreading. Emphasize that all group members share equal responsibility for accuracy in facts, grammar, and spelling.

COMMENTS/NOTES

If students have not previously studied the newspaper as a communication medium, discuss the reason for different features in a newspaper. Help them understand that a variety of features broadens the appeal of a paper to a wider range of readers.

Background. Some common themes that dominated the 1920s decade include: *fear of aliens* (such as the Red Scare and immigration restriction), *defiance of social and cultural traditions* (such as new clothing styles, jazz), *lawlessness* (such as rise of organized crime and bootlegging), *urban-rural tension* (such as the Scopes Trial), *consumerism* (such as buying on credit, use of advertising), and *religious revivalism* (such as the Billy Sunday meetings).

If students have access to a computer, you may want to encourage them to design and compose their newspapers on it.

4. If you plan to allow class time for groups to assemble their final products, point out that students will need to bring all the components (including drawings, photos, and photocopies) they plan to use. If they wish to use special art supplies, they will need to bring them.

Concluding

Display students' completed newspapers and allow time for class members to review each other's work. Conclude the activity by asking students to describe the major themes of the 1920s reflected in the newspapers. Call on volunteers to describe why they would or would not like to have lived during the time period. Ask class members to compare and contrast the 1920s with the present decade.

Evaluating Student Work

Each student may be evaluated on group participation and on the group's newspaper.

- Criteria for evaluating group participation may include contribution of ideas, cooperation in giving and receiving assignments, and meeting group deadlines.
- Criteria for evaluating students' newspapers may include coverage of all assigned topics, accuracy, neatness and attractiveness in design and layout, creativity, and meeting of requirements listed on Activity Sheet 20.

A reasonable expectation of length for a newspaper is 4–6 sheets of poster paper.

All the News That's Fit to Print
Planning a Newspaper on the 1920s

The Project

Your task is to create a newspaper that presents information about the 1920s. Your newspaper must include news articles, pictures, editorials, advertisements, classified advertisements, sports columns, fashion news, and cartoons. It is to include information for the entire decade, not just a single day or year.

Create your newspaper by working in your assigned group. Each member is responsible for four assignments—two major articles or editorials and two features, including pictures, maps, and graphs if necessary. Topics are listed below. Each article/editorial topic should be reported by only one writer, but more than one writer may do the same kind of feature. For instance, there may be two sports columns as long as they are on different topics. You may choose other topics with your teacher's approval.

Major Articles or Editorials

Morals and values
Prohibition
Fads/heroes
Flappers
Stock market investment
The "Red Scare"
The Scopes Trial
The influence of the KKK
Impact of the automobile
Crime/gangsters
Lindbergh's flight
Farmers

Features

Clothing/fashion column
Music column
Sports column
Editorial cartoon
Classified advertisements
Column on new consumer products
Radio program review
Movie review
Book review
Letter to the editor

You may look for information in your text, other history books, encyclopedias, and historical fiction. You may need to do research in the school or public library. All articles, editorials, and features must be typed or printed and written in a journalistic style with correct grammar and spelling. When the individual pieces are complete, the group will compile them on poster paper in newspaper format. To meet minimum requirements, your newspaper must have:

- a name.
- recognizable sections (such as news, editorial, cartoons, sports).
- headlines and bylines for all articles and features.
- appropriate illustrations, photographs, charts, and graphs.
- carefully proofed copy.
- an attractive, neat design and layout.

I Remember the Great Depression
Conducting an Oral History Interview

About the Activity

Students may think that the Great Depression is ancient history. This activity challenges that perception by having them interview someone who lived through the 1930s. The activity is most effective after students have studied the period.

After participating in the activity, students will be able to

- plan, conduct, and record an oral history interview.
- compare text and reference book descriptions of the Great Depression with descriptions by depression survivors.
- identify key values that depression-era survivors formed during the 1930s and maintain today.

Planning for the Activity

Suggested Time: part of 1 class period to assign project, out-of-class interview time, 1 to 2 class periods for discussion

Materials: Activity Sheet 21, one per student

THE ACTIVITY

Getting Started

Begin by asking students to describe ways in which historians collect information about past events and people (reading primary and secondary sources, interviewing people who lived during the time). Point out that information gathered in interviews and based on personal recollections is called oral history. Have class members list benefits and drawbacks to oral histories as a source of historical information.

Teaching

Explain to the class that in this activity they will conduct oral-history interviews with people who lived through the Great Depression. Emphasize that such interviews are increasingly valuable because the memories of people who lived through that era will soon be lost to history if they are not collected and preserved.

1. Distribute Activity Sheet 21 and review the directions. Be sure students understand that their interviewees must have been born before 1920 to ensure that they have extensive firsthand memories.

You may wish to allow students to tape-record their interviews, as historians do. Some students, however, may prefer to write down responses. Either way, a written summary of the answers should be required.

COMMENTS/NOTES

Background. Studs Terkel's *Hard Times* is perhaps the best-known oral history of the era.

2. Assign a due date for completed summaries of the interviews. Explain that on that date students will share their information by participating in a scored discussion.

3. On the due date, direct students to arrange their desks or chairs in a large circle. Describe the rules of a scored discussion as follows:

- Each time you contribute information to the discussion, you will receive 1 to 3 points, depending on the quality of the information and the clarity with which you present it.

- The discussion will begin with the second question on Activity Sheet 21 and follow through the rest of the questions in the order they appear. As the discussion focuses on a question for which you have interesting information or a colorful story, enter the conversation, but be careful not to monopolize the discussion.

- The first time you contribute to the discussion, begin by providing information about your interviewee's background from question 1 and his or her present-day situation.

- To participate in the discussion, you do not need to raise your hand, but if you interrupt someone you will not get points for your contribution. Be patient and courteous, offering your contributions when there is a pause in the conversation.

- Distracting or disruptive behavior while others are talking will result in the loss of two points.

4. Begin the discussion by calling on a volunteer to introduce his or her interviewee and share the responses to question 2. Continue the discussion until all questions have been addressed and all students who wish to contribute have had that opportunity.

Concluding

When students have finished discussing all 15 questions, conclude with these questions:

- What key values formed by depression-era survivors in the 1930s are still important to them today?

- What information learned from interviewees confirms or disputes information you found in the text or other resources? How might you explain any conflicting information?

- How reliable and useful do you feel oral history is in learning about a particular time period?

Evaluating Student Work

Evaluation may be based on clarity and completeness of the interview summaries and on participation in the dis-

To allow sufficient time for students to arrange for and conduct their interviews, you may wish to make this assignment over a vacation period.

Background. Although millions of people suffered severe financial losses during the Great Depression, some actually profited by buying valuable land and property at very low prices.

The scoring is, of course, intended to encourage participation. Depending on the class, though, this possible benefit should be weighed against the potential negative impact of a competitive atmosphere. The primary goal of the discussion is for students to learn about experiences of people who lived through the Great Depression. If scoring the discussion will interfere with spontaneity, you might evaluate students primarily on their written summaries.

cussion. The following tips may help you in scoring the discussion:

- Most contributions will be worth two points; short bits of information merit only one point, while longer, well-told contributions deserve three points.

- To facilitate scoring, use a photocopy of your class roster and assign points beside each student's name as the discussion progresses.

_____

_____

_____

_____

_____

I Remember the Great Depression
Interviewing a Survivor of the 1930s

Directions:

Your interviewee must have been born before 1920 so that he or she was at least ten years old in 1930. Try a family member or friend, or contact a senior center or nursing home and explain your interest in identifying an interviewee.

Make an appointment for the interview, allowing at least an hour. Take careful notes and encourage the interviewee to answer as fully as possible by probing for details and interesting stories. Add other questions to those on this sheet. Be courteous and appreciative of the interviewee's experiences and time.

Write a clear, well-organized, and complete record of the interview in preparation for a class discussion. Write a thank-you note to your interviewee.

Interview Questions

Name of Interviewee _____ Year of Birth _____

1. Where did you live during the Great Depression? With whom did you live?
2. Did you move during the depression? If so, why? Were any people you knew forced to move? Why?
3. Did you or others you knew lose jobs? What happened as a result?
4. Did you or others you knew lose homes? What was it like?
5. How did 1930s prices compare with those in the 1920s? Give some examples.
6. What did you do for medical care?
7. What did you and others do for recreation?
8. How did the depression affect your school experience?
9. How did bank closings affect you or people you knew?
10. What do you remember about "bums" and "hobos"?
11. How would you compare the attitudes and actions of Hoover and Roosevelt?
12. What are your impressions of depression-era relief programs?
13. Did you or anyone you knew prosper during the depression? Why or how?
14. What are your most vivid memories of the depression?
15. How did the depression affect your outlook on the nation and the world?

Give Us a New Deal
Answering Letters to the Government

About the Activity

No expression of Great Depression suffering was more vivid than the letters victims wrote to the newly elected President Roosevelt and members of his administration. In this activity, students read such letters and advise the President on how best to respond to the writers' concerns. This activity is most effective when used after students have studied the beginnings of the Great Depression but before they have read about the New Deal.

After participating in the activity, students will be able to

- identify problems created for average Americans by the Great Depression.
- describe ways in which the federal government proposed to meet people's needs and stabilize the nation during the depression.
- understand the significance of the New Deal.

Planning for the Activity

Suggested Time: 2 class periods

Materials: Activity Sheets 22a and 22b, one of each per student

THE ACTIVITY

Getting Started

Introduce the activity by writing the terms *Causes* and *Consequences* on the chalkboard and asking students to describe the causes and consequences of the Great Depression. List responses under the appropriate headings. Encourage students to refer to their texts.

Teaching

Explain to students that they will read copies of actual letters sent to President Roosevelt and members of his administration during the depression, describing how they have fallen victim to the depression and asking for government assistance.

1. Distribute copies of Activity Sheets 22a and 22b and review the instructions.

2. When students have finished reading the letters, divide the class into small groups. Explain that because the White House received so much mail in the 1930s, the President and his top administrators could not personally read most of the letters. They relied on readers to provide them with summaries. Ask students to imagine that they are readers, and direct them to list the problems noted in the letters.

3. Call on students from each group to identify prob-

COMMENTS/NOTES

_____

_____

_____

_____

_____

Background. Historians estimate that during his first week in office, Roosevelt received 450,000 letters. While in office, Roosevelt received an average of 5,000 to 8,000 letters per day, which were read and answered by a staff of 50 persons. Approximately 15 million letters from the public have been preserved in the Franklin D. Roosevelt Library.

_____

_____

_____

_____

_____

Background. By 1933, nearly one fourth of the nation's

lems described in the letters. List these on the chalkboard.

4. Reconvene the small groups and ask them to imagine themselves as advisors to Roosevelt. They are to prepare specific suggestions for federal programs to respond to the problems. They must be able to show how their programs will address the problems.

5. In a class discussion, call on groups to share their recommendations. Ask the following questions:

- Which problems seemed most difficult?
- Was it possible to design a single program to deal with all the problems?
- Were there any problems for which the government should not take responsibility?
- Could any problems be solved without the government spending money?

Concluding

As a concluding assignment, instruct students to write a letter to President Roosevelt. The letter should describe the problems of average Americans during the Great Depression and suggest how the federal government can best help solve them and stabilize the nation.

Encourage students to keep in mind their proposed recovery programs as they read about the New Deal.

Evaluating Student Work

Options for evaluating student work include:

- evaluating participation in discussions using criteria such as number of contributions, cooperativeness, and attentiveness.
- evaluating letters using criteria such as clarity in defining problems, quality of proposed solutions, and persuasiveness.

workers (13–14 million people) were without jobs. When these workers' families are included in the number of Americans without a regular income, the total reaches about 40 million for the year 1933.

Two letters included on the Activity Sheets are addressed to Frances Perkins, Roosevelt's Secretary of Labor. Another is addressed to Mr. Woodworth, who is thought to have been an official in the Federal Emergency Relief Administration. The secondary sources are *Slaves of the Depression: Workers' Letters About Life on the Job*, edited by Gerald Markowitz and David Rosner (Ithaca: Cornell University Press, 1967), and *Down and Out in the Great Depression: Letters from the Forgotten Man*, edited by Robert S. McElvaine (Chapel Hill: University of North Carolina Press, 1983).

You may wish to have students name and identify acronyms for the recovery programs they develop. Point out that many of the New Deal programs were best known by their acronyms.

_____

_____

_____

_____

_____

_____

_____

_____

_____

_____

Give Us a New Deal
Reading Letters to the Government

Directions:

The letters here and on Activity Sheet 22b were written to President Franklin Roosevelt or members of his administration. They reflect the concerns and needs of average Americans during the Great Depression. Spelling and punctuation are as in the original letters. Read the letters and consider what actions, if any, the federal government might take on behalf of these people and the millions of others who suffered similar problems.

Weston, Ohio, March 2, 1937

Dear Miss Perkins:

In hope that there is someway out of the situation in which we find ourselves, I'm sending you a letter. Please read & consider it.

There is help for men in almost every walk of life in America but the lowly farmhand. The farmer has his from the government, the shop worker, the railroader, in fact every working man but the farm laborer. They get nothing.

My husband works from 6 to 7 a.m. doing chores from 8 a.m. to 12 noon takes his hour then works till 6 p.m. gets $35 per mo. a very poor house to live in a garden 200 ft.sq. and 1 gal. of scimed or separated milk a day.

On this we must feed & cloth 4 children. Understand this is for 10 mo. The first of Jan. he is out of work completely.

How can this be a land of opportunity for our children if they must grow up under conditions like that? It seems to me there should be some better way for the Farm Laborer.

You see, this is only one of many cases throughout the country.

Farmers have their swell cars, their fancy meals, their nice cloths. But the man who makes their money gets scarcely enough to eat.

How can we give our children a decent chance on such conditions?

Maby you, I hope you Miss Perkins sees this instead of one of your staff looking at it and tossing it in the waste basket, can see if something can be done.

Please do something for the Farm Laborers.

In hopes of better times

Mrs. J.B.T.

Huntsville, Ala., November 12, 1935

Mr. Woodworth

Dear Sir:

I wont to know why it is we people in Huntsville are working and cant get any money or food. We white and colored people we are on a starvation. It is any way on earth you can help us we are really in need. We han't got but one check in three months. We will have to face the winter naked, hungry + nothing to go up on not even fuel to burn. we can't live + work off of nothing.

We can't get any credit to get any food or any thing families of six + seven can't get food for their kids. The kids are hungry.

I will close
From Huntsville

Sulphur Springs, Texas
December 11, 1934

President Roosevelt,
Washington, D.C.

Dear President:

I am in debt needing help the worst in the world. I own my own little home and a few live stock. Nine (9) head of red white face cattle and a span of mules. I have them all mortgaged to a man and he is fixing to foreclose me.

I have done all I could to pay the note and have failed on everything I've tried. I fell short on my crop this time and he didn't allow me even one nickle out of it to feed myself while I was gathering it and now winter is here and I have a wife and three (3) little children, haven't got clothes enough to hardly keep them from freezing. My house got burned up three years ago and I'm living in just a hole of a house and we are in a suffering condition. My little children talking about Santa Claus and I hate to see Xmas come this time because I know it will be one of the dullest Xmas they ever witnessed.

I have tried to compromise with the man that I am in debt to and he wont except nothing but the money or my stock and I can't borrow the money and I need my stock so I am asking you for help of some kind please.

So I remain,

Your humble servant,
N.S. [male]

P.S. That man won't even agree for me to have my stock fed.

Brooklyn, New York
March, 29, 1935

Dear Miss Perkins:

Reading about you as I do I have come to the understanding, that you are a fair and impartial observer of labor conditions in the United States. Well, I'll have to get a load off my chest, and tell you of the labor conditions in a place which is laughingly called a factory. We work in a Woolstock Concern. We handle discarded rags. We work, ten hours a day for six days. In the grime and dirt of a nation. We go home tired and sick—dirty—disgusted—with the world in general, work—work all day, low pay—average wage sixteen dollars. Tired in the train going home, sitting at the dinner table, to tired to even wash ourselves, what for—to keep body and souls together not to depend on charity. What of N.R.A.? What of everything—? We handle diseased rags all day. Tuberculosis roaming loose, unsanitary conditions—, slaves—slaves of the depression! I'm even tired as I write this letter—, a letter of hope—. What am I? I am young—I am twenty, a high school education—no recreation—no fun—. Pardon ma'am—but I want to live—! Do you deny me that right—? As an American citizen I ask you—, what—what must we do? Please investigate this matter. I sleep now, yes ma'am with a prayer on my lips, hoping against hope—, that you will better our conditions. I'll sign my name, but if my boss finds out—, well— Give us a new deal, Miss Perkins. The address of the concern is Simons Wool Stock, 20 Broadway, Brooklyn, N.Y.

Yours hoping,
J.G.

Hands On or Hands Off?
Debating Policies of Intervention and Isolation

About the Activity

Revolutionaries have just taken control of the fictitious nation of Marzusca. Should the United States intervene? In this activity, students debate that question as they role play isolationists and interventionists.

After participating in the activity, students will be able to

- identify major differences between the positions of interventionists and isolationists.
- describe reasons and ways that nations seek to influence or intervene in the affairs of other nations.
- evaluate the legitimacy of foreign intervention.

Planning for the Activity

Suggested Time: 2 class periods

Materials: Activity Sheets 23a and 23b, one each per student

THE ACTIVITY

Getting Started

Introduce the activity by asking students to define the terms *intervention* and *isolation* as they relate to foreign policy. Call on volunteers to provide examples, historical or recent, of the United States intervening militarily in another country. Then ask for examples of the United States choosing to remain isolated from the affairs of another country. Allow students to refer to their history texts, if necessary.

Teaching

Point out to students that during the years 1920 through 1941 Americans frequently debated the question of intervention or isolation. Explain that students will debate whether the United States, in 1933, should intervene in the internal affairs of a fictitious country.

1. Based on the examples of United States intervention in the affairs of other countries, ask students to suggest reasons why the course of intervention was taken. List responses on the chalkboard.

2. Ask students to discuss reasons why most people in the United States favored a policy of isolationism in world affairs after World War I. List reasons on the chalkboard.

3. Distribute copies of Activity Sheet 23a to all students and ask them to read both committee descriptions on the sheet.

4. Randomly assign half the class to role-play members

COMMENTS/NOTES

Background. Although most Americans preferred a policy of isolationism after World War I, the United States, adhering to the Monroe Doctrine, was very involved in the affairs of several Latin American countries. See Additional Background Information.

Background. Some conditions under which military intervention has been justified are: evidence of human rights violations, armed aggression, nationalization of foreign-owned business, threats of harm to American citizens in foreign countries, refusal to repay foreign loans, disruption of import/export markets, destruction of natural resources, and disruption of regional stability.

of the Farewell to Arms committee and the other half to role-play Worldwide Freedom committee members. Divide the two committees into small groups of four or five students each.

5. Distribute copies of Activity Sheet 23b and ask students to read the description of Marzusca. Explain that they are to assume their role as members of the Farewell to Arms or the Worldwide Freedom committees as they develop, within their small groups, a short presentation in which they argue for or against United States intervention in the affairs of Marzusca. They should also be prepared to engage in a debate on the issue after giving their presentations.

6. Have each group choose one member to present the group's position. Begin with a presentation supporting United States intervention in Marzusca. Follow with a presentation against intervention. Rotate "for" and "against" presentations until all small groups have been represented.

7. Following the formal presentations, open the discussion to the class and have them continue to debate the proper action for the United States to take in Marzusca.

Concluding

After students have finished discussing the Marzusca case study, ask the following questions:

- Other than military intervention, how might one nation intervene in or seek to influence the internal affairs of another nation?
- Which policy—intervention, or isolationism— should the United States generally follow in the world today? What specific circumstances might influence the policy choice?

Evaluating Student Work

To evaluate participation in the group discussions, use criteria such as demonstrated understanding of basic foreign policy concepts, participation in presentation planning, clear expression of ideas, and use of persuasive arguments.

As an optional evaluation, assign students to develop an American foreign policy position they believe would be viable in today's world. Direct them to "create" a new organization to promote the policy, giving the organization a name and writing a one-page summary of its rationale and policy recommendations.

Additional Background Information

In 1921 United States military forces were stationed in the Dominican Republic, Haiti, and Nicaragua. However, in 1927 Congress rejected a plan to send U.S. forces to Mexico. The Clark Memorandum of 1930 stated that the United States had no right to intervene militarily in the affairs of Latin American nations. Although revolutions took place in Brazil in 1930 and in Panama, Cuba, and Honduras in 1931, the United States did not intervene. In 1933 President Roosevelt, under the "Good Neighbor Policy," began to withdraw troops from Latin America. In 1935 American troops were withdrawn from Haiti, giving Latin America freedom from American military influence for the first time since 1898. The United States also exercised a policy of nonmilitary intervention in Asia, Europe, and the Pacific after the end of World War I.

Hands On or Hands Off?
Identifying Positions of Isolationists and Interventionists

Directions:

Read the following descriptions and prepare to role-play membership in one of the two committees.

The Committee for a Farewell to Arms

Your committee has named itself after the 1929 Ernest Hemingway novel *A Farewell to Arms*. Your group is actively involved in supporting world peace, disarmament, and isolationism. You believe that diplomacy is the principal means for resolving international conflict, and that only through diplomacy can peace and security for all nations be maintained. Farewell to Arms also asserts that money spent on acquiring arms and fighting wars could be better spent on domestic programs for United States citizens needing public assistance.

The Committee for Worldwide Freedom

The Committee for Worldwide Freedom believes in maintaining a strong United States military force. This force is necessary, according to your group, because military intervention is sometimes the only means to establish and maintain long-term peace and security for all nations. Your group is not just concerned about American citizens. It believes that our country has an obligation to protect the rights of all people to choose freedom. Your group asserts that simply the threat of military intervention will deter most challenges to freedom. When threats are not sufficient, the committee advocates military intervention to remind others of this nation's commitment to freedom and the democratic process.

Hands On or Hands Off?
Debating U.S. Policy in Marzusca

Directions:

Read the following case study and be prepared to argue for or against United States intervention in Marzusca in 1933.

Trouble in Marzusca

Marzusca is a small tropical country in Central America with a population of 5.2 million people. Seventy-five percent of the population lives in rural areas where the primary economic activity is agriculture. Marzusca exports 55 percent of its agricultural products to the United States and receives from the United States 40 percent of its imports, mostly consumer goods and farm machinery. The Marzusca government is currently $2 billion in debt to the United States.

Marzusca is a poor country. Twelve percent of its labor force is unemployed, and its literacy rate is only 60 percent. Most Marzuscans—98 percent—are Mestizo, a racial mix of Indian and European backgrounds. The official national language is Spanish, and 98 percent of the population is Roman Catholic.

Today Marzusca's government is a democratic republic. Once a colony of Spain, Marzusca was granted independence in 1821. It adopted its current constitution in 1900. Several political parties vie for power in Marzusca. The most recent elected government came to power in 1928 in a free election closely supervised by officials from the United States. This Marzuscan government has been very friendly toward the United States.

In the mid 1920s, officials from the Marzuscan government invited Americans to invest in and develop copper mines and oil fields in their country. Several United States citizens invested millions of dollars in these industries. Two of the industries now employ large numbers of Marzuscan workers, along with more than 5,000 United States citizens who moved to Marzusca to work in the American-owned businesses. Marzusca is also of interest to the United States because it serves as a "buffer" between Mexico and several totalitarian governments south of Marzusca.

In August 1933 the Marzuscan military overthrew the country's elected government. A military leader, General Salazara, has assumed political power in the country. Announcing that he plans to seize all U.S. property in Marzusca, Salazara has cancelled all debts owed the United States and stopped all trade with the United States. Reports are circulating that former Marzuscan government officials have been tortured and killed by Salazara's followers. The general has stated publicly that he seeks to build closer relations with the totalitarian governments south of his country. Two days ago he ordered all United States citizens to leave Marzusca within one week.

QUESTION: What policy should the United States follow in response to these recent developments in Marzusca?

About the Activity

Should a Japanese American sign a loyalty oath to gain release from a World War II internment camp? Through a role play, students grapple with this personal dilemma.

After participating in the activity, students will be able to

- identify motivations for a society to require certain individuals or groups to sign loyalty oaths.
- evaluate the effectiveness of loyalty oaths in ensuring national security.
- recognize why some people refuse to sign loyalty oaths.

Planning for the Activity

Suggested Time: 1 class period

Materials: Activity Sheets 24a and 24b, one each per student

Advance Preparation: If students have not studied the attack on Pearl Harbor and the United States' subsequent entry into World War II, share with them the Additional Background Information on page 120 before beginning the activity.

THE ACTIVITY

Getting Started

Ask students to imagine that they have all been offered excellent jobs. To secure their jobs, however, they must take an oath of loyalty to the United States. Distribute copies of Activity Sheet 24a and read the oath aloud. Ask students for their reactions to the oath. Do they feel it is appropriate for an employer to require them to take such an oath?

Teaching

Explain to the class that the oath they just read is one that all state and local government employees in the state of Nebraska were required to affirm in 1943 as a condition of employment. Point out that while loyalty oaths were commonly required in the years during and between World War I and World War II, they posed a particular dilemma for Japanese Americans forced into internment camps after the beginning of World War II.

1. Distribute copies of Activity Sheet 24b. Review the directions and allow time for students to read the dilemma and answer the question at the bottom of the page. Emphasize that they must write at least one supporting reason for their position.

2. Divide the class into small groups of students who share the same position on whether to sign the loyalty

COMMENTS/NOTES

_____

_____

_____

_____

_____

_____

_____

_____

_____

_____

Background. On December 7, 1941, the Japanese-American Citizens' League sent the following telegram message to President Roosevelt: IN THIS SOLEMN HOUR WE PLEDGE OUR FULLEST COOPERATION TO YOU, MR. PRESIDENT, AND TO OUR COUNTRY. THERE CANNOT BE ANY QUESTION. THERE MUST BE NO DOUBT. WE, IN OUR HEARTS, ARE AMERICANS– LOYAL TO AMERICA. WE MUST PROVE THAT TO ALL OF YOU.

An alternative strategy is to form groups in which members hold differing views on whether to sign the loyalty oath. In

117

oath. Direct the groups to spend about 10 minutes comparing their reasons and preparing a case for their position to present to the class.

3. Reconvene the class and conduct a large group discussion on the dilemma. Encourage students to challenge the reasoning of classmates with whom they disagree, but insist that they refer to the text or other authoritative sources to support their arguments.

4. To conclude the discussion, take a poll of how many students would have signed the loyalty oath and how many would have refused to sign.

5. Debrief the discussion using these questions:

- What are the strongest reasons for and against signing the loyalty oath?
- Do you believe a loyalty oath is an effective way to prove a person's patriotism or loyalty?
- Was the internment a violation of Japanese Americans' rights under the Constitution? (You may wish to note that in the 1944 case *Korematsu* v. *United States* the Supreme Court upheld the policy of internment on grounds of national security.)
- Neither German Americans nor Italian Americans were ever relocated or required, as a group, to sign loyalty oaths. Why do you think Japanese Americans were treated differently?
- In 1988 Congress passed legislation to formally apologize to Japanese Americans for the internment during World War II and to provide a monetary compensation of $20,000 to each former internee. Do you think this was an appropriate action?
- Do you think internment based on race could happen again? Explain.

Concluding

Conclude by asking students to imagine themselves as Japanese Americans in an internment camp and to write letters to President Roosevelt explaining why they will or will not sign the loyalty oath. In their letters, students should review the history of Japanese internment as well as state their opinions on oaths as a test of loyalty. Although letters are to be based on fact, they should be written in a personal, persuasive style.

Evaluating Student Work

Students may be evaluated on their group participation and their letters.

- Criteria for evaluating group participation may include attentiveness to the specifics of the dilemma, contributions to group deliberation, and willingness to take and support a stand.

these groups, students should compare the reasons for their differing opinions.

_____

_____

_____

_____

Background. *Issei,* the term for first generation, refers to native-born Japanese who immigrated to the United States. *Nisei* is the term for second-generation Japanese Americans, who are American citizens by birth.

_____

_____

_____

_____

_____

_____

_____

_____

You may wish to have students compare instances of "Japan-bashing" in the 1990s with the internment mentality of the 1940s.

_____

_____

_____

_____

_____

_____

_____

_____

- Criteria for evaluating letters may include accuracy in stating the history of Japanese-American internment, clarity in stating a position, and persuasiveness in defending that position.

_____

_____

_____

Additional Background Information

As tension heightened between the United States and Imperial Japan in the 1930s, Japanese Americans increasingly found their loyalty to the United States questioned. Though most Japanese Americans were Nisei, that is, American citizens by birth, they were suspected of being "un-American." By the eve of the attack on Pearl Harbor, there was a pervasive belief, fueled by nativism and racism, that Japanese Americans could not be trusted.

On February 19, 1942, President Roosevelt signed Executive Order 9066 authorizing the army to evacuate all "persons of Japanese ancestry"—citizen and alien alike—from the West Coast. Although United States military intelligence knew by the end of June 1942 that the Battle of Midway had removed the threat of Japanese invasion of Hawaii or the West Coast, at least 110,000 Japanese Americans were relocated to internment camps spread throughout the western United States.

Internees could gain freedom from the camps to take civilian jobs or serve in the military. To do so, however, they had to pass a security check, which involved having personal records checked by the FBI and filling out questionnaires that supposedly tested their loyalty. Two questions caused particular confusion and conflict:

> *No. 27. Are you willing to serve in the armed forces of the United States on combat duty, wherever ordered?*
> *No. 28. Will you swear unqualified allegiance to the United States of America and faithfully defend the United States from any or all attack by foreign or domestic forces, and forswear any form of allegiance or obedience to the Japanese emperor, to any other foreign government, power, or organization?*

Though designed primarily for Nisei men, these questions were also asked of women and Issei, many of whom were puzzled by them and therefore cautious in responding. Many women thought that if they answered yes to question 27 they might be drafted for combat duty. Some men and women, both Nisei and Issei, answered no to both questions because they were angry with the way their government was treating them. About 7,600 internees answered no to questions 27 and 28. Few of these were even potentially disloyal, but they were immediately labeled as such and therefore had no chance to leave the camps.

Most internees who were allowed to leave the camps were Nisei men. Many of them volunteered for combat duty in Europe with the famous 442 Regimental Combat Team, one of the most decorated units in United States military history.

Not until January 2, 1945 were the camps officially closed. In 1948 Congress passed the Japanese-American Evacuation Claims Act, which provided token compensation for evacuees' losses, approximately ten cents on the dollar.

Why Do I Have to Prove My Loyalty?
Taking an Oath of Loyalty

I, _____, do solemnly swear that I will support and defend the Constitution of the United States and the Constitution of this State, against all enemies, foreign and domestic; that I will bear true faith and allegiance to the same; that I take this obligation freely, without any mental reservation or for purpose of evasion; and that I will faithfully and impartially perform the duties of my office according to law, and to the best of my ability, and I do further swear that I do not advocate, nor am I a member of any political party or organization that advocates the overthrow of the government of the United States or of this state by force or violence; and that during such time as I am in this position I will not advocate nor become a member of any political party or organization that advocates the overthrow of the government of the United States or of this state by force or violence. So help me God.

Why Do I Have to Prove My Loyalty?
Resolving a Personal Dilemma

Directions:

Imagine yourself in the following situation, which was faced by many Japanese Americans in internment camps during World War II. Then answer the question. Be prepared to discuss and defend your answer.

You are one of over 100,000 West Coast Japanese Americans who were placed in internment camps in 1942. President Roosevelt, who said he feared internal violence and subversion during the early part of World War II, signed Executive Order 9066 authorizing the Army to evacuate "all persons of Japanese ancestry"—both citizen and alien alike. By November 1942 all West Coast Japanese Americans had been placed in camps. The government claimed the action was necessary to protect the Japanese Americans as well as to ensure the safety of the country.

You are a Nisei, an American citizen by birth. You believe that being forced to live in a hastily built bar-racks surrounded by barbed-wire fence violates your civil rights. You know that some persons have been allowed to leave the camp after they promised to move into the interior of the country. To get permission to leave, you will have to complete a questionnaire that includes a loyalty oath in the form of this question:

> *Will you swear unqualified allegiance to the United States of America and faithfully defend the United States from any or all attack by foreign or domestic forces, and forswear any form of allegiance or obedience to the Japanese emperor, to any other foreign government, power, or organization?*

You are not sure what to do. On the one hand, you question whether you can truthfully answer "yes" after the way the United States government has treated you. Also, by forswearing allegiance to Japan, you believe you would be indicating that you once had allegiance to Japan, which is not true. On the other hand, signing the oath seems to be the only way to get your family out of the camp, with its crowded living conditions and limited opportunities. Adding to your dilemma are reports of anti-Japanese sentiment in much of the country. You wonder how safe you and your family would be outside of the internment camp.

QUESTION: How would you answer the loyalty question? Provide at least one reason for your answer.

The Marshall Plan: Enlightened Self-Interest?
Ranking Rationales for Aid to Europe

About the Activity

Why would a victor give massive aid to its defeated enemies as well as its allies? Students learn in this activity that the Marshall Plan posed questions similar to those asked today about the purpose and value of foreign aid.

After participating in the activity, students will be able to

- identify and explain several rationales for the Marshall Plan.
- defend a rationale for foreign aid at the end of World War II.
- recognize domestic and international needs as competing interests in government spending.

Planning for the Activity

Suggested Time: 1 class period

Materials: Activity Sheets 25a and 25b, one each per student

THE ACTIVITY

Getting Started

Begin by asking students to write their answer to this question: Why did the United States offer massive economic aid to European nations following World War II? Compare their answers, posting the responses on the chalkboard.

Teaching

Explain to the class that the purpose of this activity is to examine and evaluate rationales put forth in support of the post-World War II Marshall Plan.

1. Distribute copies of Activity Sheets 25a and 25b and ask students to read the directions and four rationales. Have them rank the rationales, with number 1 being the most compelling.

2. Divide the class into groups of five or six students. Instruct members of each group to compare their individual rankings of the rationales. Explain that each group must come to an agreement on a ranking.

3. When students have reached agreement, ask a representative from each group to post that ranking on the chalkboard. Compare the rankings, noting the rationales identified as most and least compelling. Allow groups to justify their rankings to other class members.

4. Extend the discussion with these questions:

- Was the Marshall Plan an example of American self-interest or selflessness? Explain.

COMMENTS/NOTES

If students have not studied the Marshall Plan, allow them time to read the relevant information in their text.

Background. George C. Marshall, who had been army chief of staff during World War II, served as President Truman's secretary of state from 1947 to 1949. Marshall outlined the Marshall Plan, officially known as the European Recovery Program, in a commencement address at Harvard University on June 5, 1947.

Define *rationale* as an explanation of the underlying reasons for a particular belief or action.

Emphasize that the rationales for implementing the Marshall Plan were particularly important to congressional representatives who had to vote to appropriate funds for the program at a time when there were great needs at home.

- What, if any, debt of gratitude should the nations of Europe feel toward the United States for the Marshall Plan?

- Some people today believe the United States should implement "Marshall Plans" for Central America and regions of Africa. Would you support providing massive amounts of aid to address economic problems of these or other parts of the world? Explain.

Concluding

Emphasize that the Marshall Plan is an example of the United States providing help to people in other nations. Point out that our country continues to be called upon to help people in other nations and that sometimes financial constraints force our government to choose between meeting the needs of people at home and those of people in foreign countries.

Direct students to write editorials expressing their opinions on the proper balance between foreign and domestic spending. Have them address their editorials to members of Congress, who are responsible for appropriating funds for programs like the Marshall Plan.

Evaluating Student Work

Students' work may be evaluated on group participation and the editorials.

- Criteria for evaluating group work may include level of participation, strength of arguments for rankings, and members' willingness to help reach group consensus.

- Criteria for evaluating editorials may include clarity in expressing the position, specificity in supporting arguments, and persuasiveness.

The Marshall Plan: Enlightened Self-Interest?
Ranking Rationales for Aid to Europe

Directions:

Imagine you are American citizens in 1947. As you read about the terrible postwar economic conditions in Europe, you also have very real concerns about the actions and motives of the Soviet Union and its leader, Joseph Stalin. During the war you called Stalin "Uncle Joe" and considered him our ally. In the last few months, however, a more threatening side of Stalin has appeared. Communism has spread into the Eastern European nations, and you wonder if it will spread further.

At home you know the economy has to adjust from its high levels of wartime production. You wonder if there will be jobs for returning soldiers, and what will happen to the people who worked in the war production factories. You hear on June 5, 1947, that Secretary of State George C. Marshall has offered generous economic aid to the war-torn nations of Europe. He has presented several rationales, or explanations of reasons, for extending this aid.

On this sheet and Activity Sheet 25b are four rationales for the Marshall Plan. Read them and rank them from most to least compelling. Be prepared to explain your ranking.

Rationale 1: Stabilizing Western Democracies in Europe

Without question, the wartime alliance between the United States and the Soviet Union was one of convenience, based on defeating a common and terrible foe. With the defeat of Hitler and the Nazi state, distrust between the United States and Soviet Union has quickly returned. Of greatest concern to the United States is the belief that Stalin seeks control of Western Europe. Democratic governments in Western Europe are struggling to provide for their people in the wake of the war's devastation. At the same time, Communists are asserting that communism is the best form of government for meeting the needs of the hungry and homeless. European Communists fought fascism valiantly during the war, and they claim the right to participate in forming postwar governments. Stalin will probably back their claims, and revolutions and civil wars may occur. The United States is clearly unwilling to send an American occupation army to ensure European stability. Therefore, the next best action is to give the European democracies massive amounts of economic aid. By so doing, the United States will protect Europe from becoming a "seedbed" for Communist revolution and strengthen the infant democracies.

The Marshall Plan: Enlightened Self-Interest?
Ranking Rationales for Aid to Europe

Rationale 2: Fighting the Spread of International Communism

With the end of World War II in Europe, Stalin's powerful Red Army is in control of the Eastern European nations. While Stalin might argue that this is a small payment for the 20 million Russians who died and the massive suffering his nation experienced during the war, it appears that gaining control of Eastern Europe is just one part of an effort to spread communism throughout the world. That effort has to be resisted whenever and wherever necessary. The struggle can be summed up as one between two opposing systems: capitalist democracy and communist totalitarianism. Our best weapon in the battle against world communism is our powerful capitalist economy and the economic aid we can provide to Europe's struggling democracies. The Marshall Plan represents a strong response to counter the plan of Joseph Stalin to increase his control over Europe and, ultimately, to spread communism around the world.

Rationale 3: Promoting Our Economic Growth

World War II saw the destruction of nearly 70 percent of Europe's industry and 60 percent of its transportation system. Today, Europe's economy is in ruins. Meanwhile, the United States has an enormous economic capacity, developed to meet wartime production needs. However, the United States now faces the prospect of a serious economic downturn because war production is ending faster than new markets can be found. One possibility for continuing a healthy pace of economic growth in the United States is to establish new markets in Europe and elsewhere. The Marshall Plan will give Europeans money they can use to buy American agricultural, industrial, and consumer goods. By linking Europe's economy to ours, we will prevent serious economic problems here in the United States while helping rebuild the European economy.

Rationale 4: Providing Humanitarian Aid To Those In Need

The nations of Europe suffered unparalleled hardship and destruction during World War II. Now that the war is over, there is a clear and pressing need to help in peace the peoples we helped in war. We fought to free the nations of Europe from the oppression of Nazi Germany. Surely it is only right to provide economic assistance to those who now return to bombed-out cities and war-ravaged fields. It would be "un-American" to turn our backs on our distant relatives who now face hunger, homelessness, and the difficult task of rebuilding the lives they once knew.

McCarthyism and "Dirty Politics"
Distinguishing Between Ethical and Unethical Politics

About the Activity

What kind of politics is "dirty"? Who distinguishes between political right and wrong? This activity requires students to draw an ethical line in a case study of political ethics.

After participating in the activity, students will be able to

- describe the political intent and strategies associated with McCarthyism.
- evaluate the ethical issues in a political case study.

Planning for the Activity

Suggested Time: 1 class period

Materials: Activity Sheet 26, one per student

THE ACTIVITY

Getting Started

Begin with a word-association challenge. Write the phrase *dirty politics* on the chalkboard. Direct students to write down the words, phrases, or images that first come to their minds when they read the phrase.

After a few minutes, call on students to share their word associations. List their answers on the chalkboard and then review the responses to identify common themes that run through their perceptions of dirty politics. List the themes.

Teaching

Explain that in this activity students will examine ethical and unethical behavior of politicians. Point out that the 1950s era of Senator Joseph McCarthy is often cited as one of our most notorious periods of dirty politics.

1. Allow students time to refer to their texts to review the political activities of McCarthy. Share the Additional Background Information about McCarthy on page 129 and ask them to summarize his political goals and strategies. Have students identify the nature of the unethical politics known as McCarthyism.

2. Challenge students to identify more recent examples of unethical political behavior by politicians.

3. Distribute copies of Activity Sheet 26 to each student. Instruct them to read the directions and the description of the dilemma.

4. Divide the class into small groups of four or five.

COMMENTS/NOTES

McCarthyism generally refers to the use of unsupported accusations to intimidate people and gain unstated political ends.

Examples of more recent unethical political behavior might include Watergate, the Iran-contra Affair, the 1990s Savings and Loan scandal, and state or local scandals.

Instruct the small groups to share and discuss the recommendations they would make to Harold Wise and then to develop a campaign strategy to deal with the baseball ownership issue. Have groups appoint a spokesperson to present their strategy to the the class.

5. Reconvene the class and call on the group spokespersons to present their campaign strategies. Encourage other students to challenge the reasoning underlying the recommendations. After all presentations have been made, review the campaign strategies and identify the most commonly recommended "should do" and "should not do" actions.

6. Pose the following questions:

- What options did Harold Wise have?
- What questions might Wise legitimately raise regarding Fillmore?
- What accusations about Fillmore might be called "dirty politics"? Why?
- What determines whether a politician's actions reflect a conflict of interest?
- Is it ever acceptable for a politician to act out of self-interest?
- Should politicians be held to higher ethical standards than other citizens?

Concluding

Write the following quotation on the chalkboard: *"Be ye therefore clever as a serpent and innocent as doves."* Tell students that the quotation is from the German philosopher Immanuel Kant. In it he suggests that politicians need to be resourceful, astute, intelligent, and powerful, but that they must also be ethical and prudent.

As a final assignment, direct students to write short essays discussing whether it is necessary for politicians to behave like both serpents and doves.

Evaluating Student Work

You may evaluate students on both their participation in group work and their essays.

- Group work evaluation criteria may include cooperativeness in discussing and supporting reasons for the recommendations to Harold Wise and willingness to challenge other students' reasoning.
- Essay evaluation criteria may include accuracy in presenting facts, clarity in identifying a position, and persuasiveness in arguments.

Background. Immanuel Kant was a German philosopher who lived in the 1700s and advocated the notion that doing one's duty is more important than being happy or making other people happy.

Background. Kant believed that the serpent and dove could coexist. In a twist on Kant's quotation, Woody Allen suggests in his book *Without Feathers* that the serpent and the doves shall lie down together, but the doves won't get much sleep.

Additional Background Information

Joseph McCarthy was elected senator from the state of Wisconsin in 1946. Before becoming a senator, he had worked as a lawyer and circuit judge, and served as a first lieutenant in the United States Marine Corps. As a senator, McCarthy was known to be arrogant and wildly unpredictable. He showed little regard for the truth, manipulated evidence, misquoted sources, and launched vicious attacks on people who challenged him.

When seeking reelection in 1952, McCarthy began his famous investigation of communism and subversion in government. McCarthy's accusations and tactics proved extremely controversial. His investigations of Communists in government were carried out in the State Department, the CIA, and the United States Army. His tactics included unsubstantiated accusations, personal attacks, vilification, misrepresentation, and diversion. Finally, in 1954 McCarthy was formally censured by the Senate. Between 1954 and 1957 he was virtually ignored by his Senate colleagues. When he spoke on the Senate floor, other senators left the chambers. McCarthy died in May 1957 at Bethesda Naval Hospital.

McCarthyism and "Dirty Politics"
Advising a Politician on Political Ethics

Directions:

Read the following description and then answer the question that follows. Be prepared to discuss your ideas with others in a small group discussion.

Mayor George Fillmore is a popular first-term mayor in a large city on the East Coast. Age 45, married, and father of two children, he was elected three years ago by an overwhelming majority. His popularity as a former star pitcher for a major league baseball team, his "common person" background, and his reputation for speaking out against injustice, corruption, and elitism were keys to his victory.

He is credited with accomplishing much as mayor, including increasing the number of jobs by bringing new business and industry to town. He helped gain funding for a new convention center and supported improving parks and playgrounds. He has brought various ethnic and cultural groups together and established a Mayor's Advisory Board to hear community concerns.

Fillmore is preparing to run for a second term. The election is six months away. His chief opponent, Harold Wise, is campaigning on promises of financial responsibility and lower taxes. Recent polls show Wise gaining in popularity. Responding that city finances are in excellent shape, Fillmore has proposed more new projects. His campaign slogan is "Let's Finish the Job!"

As part of his campaign, Fillmore has promised to improve the economy by helping to bring a major league baseball team to the city. He has announced that he has been approached by the owners of a recently purchased team. They will move the team if the city contributes land and 25 million dollars for a stadium.

After beginning discussions with the seven team owners, Fillmore learned that one of them is a former professional baseball player who for several months had played on the same team with him. The two barely knew each other during their playing days and have had no contact since then, until now. Fillmore has seen no need to publicly acknowledge that they had once been teammates. Harold Wise, though, is asking his political advisors whether this information should be used against Fillmore in the campaign.

QUESTION: If you were in a position to advise Wise, what recommendations would you make?

About the Activity

In this activity students learn about the 1960s counterculture by engaging in a scavenger hunt to find artifacts from the period.

After participating in the activity, students will be able to

- define the term *counterculture* as it was applied in the late 1960s and early 1970s.
- identify examples of the counterculture during the period.
- compare the youth counterculture of the late 1960s with their own youth culture.

Planning for the Activity

Suggested Time: 1 to 2 class periods, plus homework

Materials: Activity Sheet 27, one per student; poster paper, one sheet per two students; color marking pens

Advance Preparation: This activity is most effective after students have read about the 1960s and early 1970s in their text or other references.

THE ACTIVITY

Getting Started

Begin the activity by writing the word *culture* on the chalkboard and asking students to define it. After they arrive at a definition, ask students to give examples of culture groups in the United States today and discuss aspects of their ways of life that define them as culture groups.

Teaching

Explain that one of the significant movements in recent United States history was the emergence of a counterculture in the late 1960s. This counterculture, led and dominated by young people, challenged the traditional lifestyles and values of the middle class.

1. Discuss the concept of *counterculture*. Ask students to consider whether their own youth culture might be considered a counterculture. Identify ways in which their youth culture contrasts with the cultural norms of their parents, teachers, or other adults, and of members of their grandparents' generation. Identify ways in which their culture reflects or adheres to adult norms.

2. Tell students that to learn more about the counterculture of the late 1960s and early 1970s, they will go on a two-part scavenger hunt. First, they will identify and interview people who were in high school or college between 1966 and 1972. They should ask interviewees about characteristics of the counterculture and how those

NOTES/COMMENTS

A simple definition of *culture* is "the ways of life of a specific group of people." Ways of life include aspects such as food, dress, recreation, modes of communication, values, family structure, and religion.

characteristics challenged traditional values and lifestyles. Then they will find and bring to class an "artifact" that represents the counterculture of that period. Distribute copies of Activity Sheet 27 and review the directions with students. Set a due date.

3. On the assigned date, have students move their desks into a large circle with a table in the center. Have them place their objects on the table.

4. Call on students to begin their presentations. Direct each one to first summarize the interviews and then to show and describe the artifact. Each student should clearly state the significance of the artifact as a representation of the counterculture.

5. When all presentations have been made, ask students to analyze the artifacts and record on notebook paper generalizations about the counterculture suggested by the objects.

6. Discuss students' generalizations and then ask the following questions:

- How have your assumptions about the counterculture of the late 1960s and early 1970s been supported or challenged by this activity?
- What alternatives and variations existed within the "revolution" referred to as the counterculture?
- What objects best represent the counterculture?
- The counterculture largely reflected a "generation gap." What evidence of this generation gap did you find in your interviews and scavenger hunt?

Concluding

Distribute sheets of poster paper and marking pens to pairs of students. Tell the pairs that to conclude this activity they are to make a two-panel cartoon that compares the youth counterculture of the 1960s–1970s with their own youth culture. Encourage them to include objects representing both cultures in their illustrations. Display students' finished cartoons.

Evaluating Student Work

You may assess students' work on their class presentations and their cartoons.

- Criteria for evaluating presentations may include thoughtfulness in summarizing interviews, accuracy in selecting the artifact for display and identifying its significance, and clarity in presenting the object to the class.
- Criteria for evaluating cartoons may include accuracy in representing key elements of the two cultures and clarity in comparing the two cultures.

Some examples of counterculture "artifacts" are rock albums, peace posters, photos of hippies, tie-dyed clothing, and love beads. Caution students against bringing either drug paraphernalia or irreplaceable objects to class.

Although students' cartoons should not be evaluated on artistic talent, such ability may be noted in the completed projects.

May I Borrow Your Peace Button?
Scavenging for Artifacts of the 1960s

Directions:

The directions below will lead you on a scavenger hunt to find artifacts from the counterculture of the late 1960s and early 1970s. Write the answers on separate sheets of paper and be prepared to share the results from your hunt in a class discussion.

Going on a Scavenger Hunt

1. Identify three people who were in senior high school or college between the years 1966 and 1972. List their names and where they lived during this period.

2. Based on information you learn from interviewing these people, characterize the communities and cultures in which they grew up.

3. Ask the three people what each remembers as the most important aspects of the counterculture.

4. Ask the interviewees to name at least five artifacts (objects) that for them symbolize the counterculture. List their answers.

5. Locate and bring to class one of the artifacts named by interviewees. The artifact must be a physical object that represents the counterculture. Be prepared to share the object with the class, describing how it reflected the counterculture and how it is being used today.

You Must Pass This Little Test
Experiencing the Impact of Literacy Tests

About the Activity

In this activity students experience the unfairness of the literacy tests that were designed to deny African Americans the right to vote. Students will take a test based on an actual one used in Alabama before the Voting Rights Act of 1965.

After participating in the activity, students will be able to

- describe the role of literacy tests in denying voting rights to African Americans before the Voting Rights Act of 1965.
- identify with the frustration of African Americans against whom literacy tests discriminated.

Planning for the Activity

Suggested Time: 1 class period

Materials: Activity Sheet 28, one per student

THE ACTIVITY

Getting Started

Ask students what the requirements are for voting in national, state, and local elections (being a citizen at least eighteen years old; being a resident of the state in which you vote; and, in all states except North Dakota, being registered). Then ask them if they think people should be required to take a test in order to vote. If there were to be a test, what questions do they think should be on it and why?

After students have suggested questions, tell them that they will be taking a test to determine whether they may vote. Distribute copies of Activity Sheet 28 and allow about ten minutes for completion. Have students exchange papers for grading. (See answers to the right.) Have graders record the number of wrong answers at the top of the test. Then explain that the test is pass/fail. A perfect score is passing; any wrong answer warrants a failing grade. Ask graders to indicate "pass" or "fail" at the top of the tests.

Allow students to state their opinions about whether the test is fair. Ask them to support their opinions with specific reasons.

Teaching

1. Explain that the questions are similar to ones on literacy tests required of African Americans in the South before passage of the Voting Rights Act of 1965. The tests

COMMENTS/NOTES

_____
_____
_____
_____
_____
_____
_____
_____

You may wish to heighten the activity's impact by telling students that this is a citizenship quiz which will count toward their grade. This potential for increased impact, however, should be weighed against the possibility that their resentment at being "tricked" might interfere with focusing on the purpose of the activity.

Answers for Activity Sheet 28:

1. January 3rd
2. life
3. 9
4. no
5. do affirm
6. In God We Trust
7. 2
8. militia
9. Virginia
10. Supreme Court
11. 10 miles square
12. Congress, state
13. the governor
14. the President
15. president of the Senate

were not intended to determine knowledge of government but rather to serve as a way to deny African Americans the right to vote.

2. Divide the class into small groups of four or five. Have them read appropriate sections of their text or other references to identify other ways white officials prevented African Americans from voting and denied them equal opportunities in education, jobs, and housing. Direct them to list discriminatory practices on one side of a sheet of paper. On the other side have them list some actions taken by civil rights workers to overcome discrimination.

3. Reconvene the class and call on students to share their group findings. Ask volunteers to identify the strategies that they believe were most effective in overcoming discrimination.

Concluding

Ask students to imagine themselves as an African American who has just been denied the right to vote after "failing" a literacy test. They are to write a diary entry giving their emotional reaction and also the specific reasons why they feel they have been treated unjustly. Have students end their entries by stating how they plan to respond to the wrong done to them.

Evaluating Student Work

Group participation and the diary entries may be used for assessment.

- Criteria for evaluating small group work may include participation in identifying information and thoughtfulness in linking discriminatory practices and remedies.

- Criteria for evaluating diary entries may include expression of an appropriate level of emotion and specificity in identifying the injustices of literacy testing.

Background. After the Civil War the Fifteenth Amendment gave African-American men the right to vote; African-American women received voting rights with the Nineteenth Amendment in 1920. However, literacy tests, poll taxes, and grandfather clauses limited African Americans' access to voting until the Voting Rights Act of 1965 did away with such limitations.

Background. Whites were also given literacy tests before 1965, but their tests were composed of much simpler questions.

Students' lists of actions to overcome discrimination should include constitutional amendments, court rulings, boycotts, sit-ins, freedom rides, and marches.

General Test of Civic Literacy

Directions:

Answer each question to the best of your ability.

1. A United States senator elected in a November general election takes office the following year on what date? _____

2. A person appointed to the United States Supreme Court is appointed for a _____ term.

3. When the Constitution was approved by the original states, how many states had to ratify it before it became law? _____

4. Does enumeration affect the income tax levied on citizens in various states? _____

5. Persons opposed to "swearing" when taking an oath may say instead: "I solemnly _____."

6. What words are required by law to be on all coins and paper currency of the United States?

_____

7. Money can be appropriated for the armed services for a period of only ___ years.

8. For its own security, each state has a right to form a _____.

9. Of the original 13 states, the one with the largest representation in the first Congress was

_____.

10. If a state is a party in a legal case, the Constitution states that original jurisdiction shall be in _____.

11. The Constitution limits the size of the District of Columbia to _____.

12. The only laws applying to an area in a federal arsenal are those passed by _____, provided that consent for the purchase of the land is given by the _____.

13. If a person flees from justice from one state into another, who has authority to ask for his return?

_____.

14. If the two houses of Congress cannot agree on an adjournment time, who sets the time?

_____.

15. After the presidential electors have voted, to whom do they send their vote count?

_____

You're in the Army Now!
Simulating the Vietnam War Draft

Activity **29**

About the Activity

Through this simulation, the class will share the experience of young men who faced the Vietnam War draft lottery. Students will either be "drafted" or declared exempt solely on the basis of numbers randomly assigned to their birth dates. The lottery results will be displayed on poster sheets. To enhance the impact, there will be an assignment that only those drafted will be required to do. The simulation will help students come to grips with the issues surrounding the military draft lottery.

After participating in the activity, students will be able to

- describe the workings of the Vietnam draft lottery.
- recognize the options available to men drafted in the lottery.
- identify arguments for and against conscription in the Vietnam War.

Planning for the Activity

Suggested Time: 2 class periods, one for the draft and one for discussion of draft outcomes

Materials:

366 slips of paper, numbered from 1 to 366
366 slips of paper, each with one day of the year, including February 29
2 containers to hold the slips (fishbowls, large coffee cans, or baskets)
Poster sheets to record the lottery results
Activity Sheets 29a and 29b, one of each per student

Advance Preparation:

Place the slips with numbers in one container and the slips with days of the year in the other. Prepare enough poster sheets to fit the numbers 1 through 366, allowing space to write a date next to each number as the lottery is conducted. The poster sheets should be large enough so that the numbers and dates are legible to the class as a "public record" of the lottery results.

THE ACTIVITY

Getting Started

Begin by circulating a sheet of paper and asking each student to write his or her name and birth date on it. As students fill in the sheet, explain that in the late 1960s and early 1970s birth dates became very important to young men in the United States. Ask students if they know why. Probe their knowledge of how men were selected by the government for military service in the Vietnam War. Then explain briefly how the lottery system worked.

Clarify that under the Selective Service Act the military had the right to draft, or conscript, young men between the ages of 18 and 25. Point out that while conscription had been used in other wars, it became increasingly unpopular as public support for American involvement in the Vietnam War declined.

COMMENTS/NOTES

Background. During the Vietnam War era, great emotion surrounded the assignment of lottery dates and numbers, since a low number meant almost sure military service and a high number meant little chance of being drafted. See "Additional Background Information" for other details.

139

Teaching

Explain that the class will do a simulation of the Vietnam War draft lottery.

1. Distribute Activity Sheets 29a and 29b and review them with students. Make sure that students understand the provisions for determining who will be drafted and exempted, and that they recognize the obligations of those drafted. Set a date when assignments from "draftees" are due.

- Select a student volunteer to draw a date slip from the "date" fishbowl and a second volunteer to draw a number from the "number" fishbowl. For example, July 14 might be drawn with the number 1.

- To provide a public record of the lottery outcome, record each number and its corresponding day of the year on a poster sheet. For example, if July 14 is drawn with the number 1, the information would be recorded on the poster sheet as "1—July 14."

- Continue drawing dates and numbers until all days of the year are accounted for. If you have more than one class, you may wish to save time by having each class do part of the drawing.

2. Remind the drafted students of their obligations as stated on Activity Sheets 29a and 29b. To verify individual draft statuses, check students' lottery numbers against the list of their birth dates. You may wish to mention that providing false information to the Selective Service is a criminal act and punishable by law. Similarly, persons interfering with the work of military personnel, including the duties of Selective Service officials, are subject to criminal prosecution.

Optional Extension

To heighten realism in the simulation, announce that the "draft board" will hold a special session at a designated time to hear appeals from draftees. Draftees may appeal their conscription if they can produce legitimate reasons for being exempted. For example, the passports of foreign students would provide exemption, as would documentation of certain medical conditions for other students. The draft board might be composed of other teachers.

Concluding

Encourage students to express their reactions to the simulation by asking the following questions:

- What feelings did you have during the lottery experience?

- How did the feelings of those students who were drafted compare with those who were not?

Clarify that the assignments given to "draftees" are *not* punishment. The assignments should be considered the obligations of being drafted.

Make students aware that group protests before draft boards were common during the Vietnam War. Some young men went to jail rather than accept induction. Most protests were peaceful, but some turned violent.

Background. During the Vietnam War era, people who volunteered for military service had greater choice of assignments than those who were drafted. (Hence the offer of extra credit for volunteers on Activity Sheet 29b.) Men granted Conscientious Objector status, although free from combat duty, had to fulfill an alternative service obligation.

To reinforce this activity, you may wish to invite faculty members, parents, or other community residents to discuss their personal Vietnam War draft experiences with the class.

- Was the lottery fair?
- Should females be exempted from the draft?
- What options should be available to persons having numbers 120 or lower?
- What are the advantages and disadvantages of a draft lottery?
- What alternatives could you propose for assuring that our nation has enough people to serve in the military?

On the assigned date, collect papers from students who were "drafted." Ask them to share with the class what they learned from their interviews.

Evaluating Student Work

Evaluate students' essays on how well they meet the expectations set forth in the Draft Notification Information (Activity Sheet 29a). Essays should be clearly written, provide accurate information, and present the student's opinion. Students who were not "drafted" should be evaluated on their participation in the concluding discussion. Their contributions should reflect an understanding of the issues of fairness and loyalty that arose during the Vietnam draft.

Additional Background Information

This simulation illustrates how the draft lottery determined the sequence in which males within a given age group, such as all those born in the year 1953, were called into service. Although men who drew a low draft number were most likely to be called up, they could apply to their local draft boards for special consideration, such as medical or insanity deferments or deferments to complete their college education.

The legal mechanism authorizing the draft was left in place after the Vietnam War. Thus, the 1991 Persian Gulf War raised the possibility of reinstating the draft. Had the draft been reinstated in 1991, a lottery like the one used for Vietnam War conscription would have been implemented.

You're in the Army Now!
Draft Notification Information

Follow the directions below to determine your draft status. Failure to follow all the directions will result in your liability for any and all penalties deemed necessary by government officials or their duly appointed representatives.

1. After the lottery has been completed, confirm the number drawn for your date of birth. You have full responsibility for verifying your draft status. You are also responsible for the accuracy of the birth date on file with your teacher. If you falsify your birth date, you will be immediately classified as "DRAFTED."

2. All individuals with Draft Number 120 and below are to be immediately inducted into the Army. Draftees are to read item 4 below.

3. All individuals with Draft Numbers 121 and higher are permanently relieved of any military duties to the Republic. However, interference with the official duties of military draftees will result in the immediate induction into military service of those responsible, even if they have been previously exempt. Such interference can also result in criminal penalties.

4. Individuals with Draft Numbers 120 and below are to be immediately inducted into the Army. They are responsible for discharging all of the following duties:

A. If you are a male . . .

i. Interview someone who was drafted and served in Vietnam. Find out how he felt about the draft experience and his experiences in Vietnam.

   OR

Interview someone who was eligible for the draft but did not participate in the military. Why did he not serve? What were his feelings about the draft system at the time? What draft exemptions did he or his friends use or consider?

ii. Consider your feelings about the draft. What would you have done if you had been drafted during the Vietnam War?

iii. Write a two-page paper summarizing the results of your interviews and describing your opinions on the draft lottery.

B. If you are a female, your assignment is the same as for males in items i, ii, and iii above, except that you are to assume that it is your brother or a boyfriend who has been drafted. What will you advise him to do? What are your feelings and opinions on the draft lottery system?

You're in the Army Now!
Instructions: Deferments and Voluntary Service

Provisions for Persons Seeking Draft Deferments

Draftees wishing to petition their local Draft Hearing Board for a deferment of draft status must follow the directions below:

- A draftee must describe in detail his reasons for seeking a deferment. Information may come from interviews with individuals who were granted a deferment during the Vietnam War or from written materials.

- Draftees seeking Conscientious Objector status must interview or read about an individual who was granted this status during the Vietnam War. The draftee must be prepared to explain the interviewee's experiences and justify his own request for C.O. status.

- Petitioners for a change in draft status must be prepared to present their cases to the Draft Hearing Board at the time designated and bring any relevant documents to support their petition. The Draft

  Board will meet at the following time: _____

Special Considerations for Volunteers

Those citizens who wish to contribute to the military efforts of the Republic, but were not selected by the lottery, may volunteer their services. Their task is to contribute a paper on the topics outlined in items i, ii, and iii on Form 29a. In recognition of their courage and dedication, volunteers will receive extra credit.

About the Activity

What does Watergate mean to today's young people and to adults who lived through the scandal? Students answer this question through interviews with peers and adults.

After participating in the activity, students will be able to

- identify major events associated with the Watergate scandal.
- explain the "lessons" of Watergate as related to role of the press, national security, executive privilege, power of the Constitution, and trust in government.

Planning for the Activity

Suggested Time: 2 class periods, with intervening time for students to conduct community interviews

Materials: Activity Sheets 30a through 30e, enough copies of each for one fifth of students; poster paper and marking pens

Advance Preparation: Before beginning this activity, students should have studied the basic chronology of the Watergate break-in, cover-up, and investigations.

THE ACTIVITY

Getting Started

Call on volunteers to summarize the major events of Watergate as they understand them. Ask students to identify the important issues or questions that the events of Watergate raised for the United States government and for the American people. Post students' responses on the chalkboard.

Teaching

Point out that many historians believe the Watergate episode in American history taught the United States some important lessons about our democratic form of government. Explain that in this activity, students will identify those lessons from the perspective of other young people and adults.

1. Divide the class into five equal, or nearly equal, groups. To each group, distribute copies of one of the five Activity Sheets. Explain that although each group will be studying a different issue, the groups will follow the same directions to complete the Activity Sheet tasks. Assign a due date for individual interviews to be completed and small groups to reconvene.

2. Allow time for groups to clarify and discuss their issues. Encourage students to share strategies for identifying interviewees.

3. On the date set for interview completion, reconvene

COMMENTS/NOTES

One example of a significant issue arising from Watergate is citizen trust in government.

If students have not previously conducted community interviews, discuss appropriate behavior for doing so. Emphasize the need to respect interviewees' time, listen attentively, and prepare for the interview.

the small groups and direct them to complete step 3 on their activity sheets. Advise students to compare interview information and to identify from their interview responses some common themes and insights.

4. Distribute poster paper and marking pens to groups. Set a time for students' posters to be completed.

5. When their posters are finished, have students make short presentations on them. Encourage other students to ask questions. Display the posters as students finish their study of the 1970s.

Concluding

Bring the activity to closure by discussing the following questions:

- Do you feel there are lessons to be learned from Watergate? If so, what lessons do you think are most important for the well-being of our democratic form of government?

- From your interviews, how would you characterize people's opinions about Watergate and its impact on American government and society? Did you sense a difference between the opinions of young people and those of adults?

- How would you summarize the opinions of your interviewees about President Nixon?

- Do you believe Nixon's resignation was appropriate? Do you think President Ford's pardon of Nixon was appropriate?

- How would you characterize your trust in government and elected officials at this time? Explain.

Ask students to write a letter to the editor of their local newspaper expressing an opinion on Nixon's resignation. Direct them to include in their letter a summary of the lessons learned from Watergate.

Evaluating Student Work

Assessment of students' participation can be based on their group work and their letters to the editor.

- Evaluation of group participation can include criteria such as involvement in group discussions, timely completion of interviews, and contributions to the group poster.

- Evaluation of letters to the editor can include criteria such as clarity in identifying some lessons from Watergate and a specific response to Nixon's resignation.

For more detailed evaluation of students' interviews, require them to submit their interview notes to you at the project's end.

Background. In September 1974, when President Ford granted Nixon a total pardon for all Watergate-related activities and crimes, he stated he was doing so to spare both Nixon and the country the specter of seeing an ex-President on trial and to finally put Watergate "behind us." The pardon required no admission of guilt by Nixon.

Lessons from Watergate
Considering Issues from the Scandal

Directions:

Complete the four steps below. In steps 1, 3, and 4 you are to work with members of your small group. Step 2 you will complete on your own.

1. In your small group, discuss the issues and questions raised below. Make certain each member states his or her opinion on the questions.

2. Using the questions, interview at least two students who are not in your class and two adults who were twenty years of age or older during the Watergate years. Record the interviewees' responses and be prepared to discuss them with your small group.

3. After all interviews have been conducted, reconvene your small group. Compare the responses collected in the interviews. Identify and record some common themes or insights that emerge from the interview responses.

4. On large sheets of paper, create posters that illustrate your group's issue and the themes or insights that emerged from your interviews. Make your poster accurate, informative, and creative.

Issue: National Security

President Nixon and his aides defended many of their actions as necessary for national security. The term *national security* generally refers to keeping the nation safe from the individuals or groups who might jeopardize the lives of Americans or the stability of our government.

A. How do you define *national security?*

B. Nixon claimed that release of information on White House tapes could jeopardize national security. In what ways might that have been true?

C. Do you think the risk to national security was more or less threatening than the risk of covering up a crime?

D. In current debates, policies on trade and drug testing, for example, are justified by claims that they are necessary to protect national security. How closely do you believe such matters relate to national security?

E. Identify policies and government actions that you believe may affect national security.

Lessons from Watergate
Considering Issues from the Scandal

Directions:

Complete the four steps below. In steps 1, 3, and 4 you are to work with members of your small group. Step 2 you will complete on your own.

1. In your small group, discuss the issues and questions raised below. Make certain each member states his or her opinion on the questions.

2. Using the questions, interview at least two students who are not in your class and two adults who were twenty years of age or older during the Watergate years. Record the interviewees' responses and be prepared to discuss them with your small group.

3. After all interviews have been conducted, reconvene your small group. Compare the responses collected in the interviews. Identify and record some common themes or insights that emerge from the interview responses.

4. On large sheets of paper, create posters that illustrate your group's issue and the themes or insights that emerged from your interviews. Make your poster accurate, informative, and creative.

Issue: Role of the Media

The Watergate scandal became public largely through media persistence, particularly that of two *Washington Post* reporters, Bob Woodward and Carl Bernstein. Throughout the Watergate period, President Nixon felt he was being unfairly scrutinized by the press and that the media exaggerated the situation.

A. In a democracy, how aggressive should the press be in pursuing a story with important political implications?

B. When should the public believe the press and when should it distrust the press?

C. In what ways can a government manipulate the press? How can government manipulation of the press be avoided?

D. For weeks during the summer of 1973, Americans were glued to their TV sets watching Senate and House Watergate hearings and hearing reports of what happened at the Nixon White House. Is this type of extensive television coverage in the best interests of democracy?

E. What recent examples of intensive press coverage of political events or issues can you cite? Evaluate the role of the press in each of these situations.

Lessons from Watergate
Considering Issues from the Scandal

Directions:

Complete the four steps below. In steps 1, 3, and 4 you are to work with members of your small group. Step 2 you will complete on your own.

1. In your small group, discuss the issues and questions raised below. Make certain each member states his or her opinion on the questions.

2. Using the questions, interview at least two students who are not in your class and two adults who were twenty years of age or older during the Watergate years. Record the interviewees' responses and be prepared to discuss them with your small group.

3. After all interviews have been conducted, reconvene your small group. Compare the responses collected in the interviews. Identify and record some common themes or insights that emerge from the interview responses.

4. On large sheets of paper, create posters that illustrate your group's issue and the themes or insights that emerged from your interviews. Make your poster accurate, informative, and creative.

Issue: Power of the Constitution

Many people argue that although Watergate represented one of the greatest challenges our system of government has ever faced, the Constitution worked to keep democratic principles intact. They point out that when President Nixon resigned an orderly transition of power was accomplished. The Congress and Supreme Court exercised their powers in checking and balancing the powerful executive branch. In addition, an independent and free press was able to investigate and report on all the aspects of the unfolding case.

A. Do you agree that the Constitution worked during the Watergate years? Explain. What provisions of the Constitution were upheld?

B. If a situation like the Watergate scandal were to happen today, do you think the Constitution and the press would function as well as they did some 20 years ago?

C. How do more recent government "crises," such as the Iran-contra affair, the savings-and-loan bailout, and the Clarence Thomas hearings, compare to Watergate? What Constitutional provisions were applied in these situations?

Lessons from Watergate
Considering Issues from the Scandal

Directions:

Complete the four steps below. In steps 1, 3, and 4 you are to work with members of your small group. Step 2 you will complete on your own.

1. In your small group, discuss the issues and questions raised below. Make certain each member states his or her opinion on the questions.

2. Using the questions, interview at least two students who are not in your class and two adults who were twenty years of age or older during the Watergate years. Record the interviewees' responses and be prepared to discuss them with your small group.

3. After all interviews have been conducted, reconvene your small group. Compare the responses collected in the interviews. Identify and record some common themes or insights that emerge from the interview responses.

4. On large sheets of paper, create posters that illustrate your group's issue and the themes or insights that emerged from your interviews. Make your poster accurate, informative, and creative.

Issue: Executive Privilege

Some conversations in our society are considered "privileged." Privileged means the conversations cannot be repeated, even in a court of law. Examples are conversations between lawyers and clients, doctors and patients, and priests and confessors. President Nixon claimed that conversations between the President and people who advise him or her are also privileged. He reasoned that the only way a President can get honest advice is for advisors to know that whatever is said will not be made public. When his lawyers went to court to block release of the White House tapes, they claimed executive privilege. The Supreme Court rejected their claim.

A. Do you think Nixon's claim of executive privilege should have been upheld by the Court in the Watergate case?

B. In what situations might executive privilege be legitimate?

C. How can the public's right to know and the President's need for candid advice be balanced?

D. When, if ever, should a President withhold information from the public for the public's "own good"?

Lessons from Watergate
Considering Issues from the Scandal

Directions:

Complete the four steps below. In steps 1, 3, and 4 you are to work with members of your small group. Step 2 you will complete on your own.

1. In your small group, discuss the issues and questions raised below. Make certain each member states his or her opinion on the questions.

2. Using the questions, interview at least two students who are not in your class and two adults who were twenty years of age or older during the Watergate years. Record the interviewees' responses and be prepared to discuss them with your small group.

3. After all interviews have been conducted, reconvene your small group. Compare the responses collected in the interviews. Identify and record some common themes or insights that emerge from the interview responses.

4. On large sheets of paper, create posters that illustrate your group's issue and the themes or insights that emerged from your interviews. Make your poster accurate, informative, and creative.

Issue: Trust in Government

The Watergate scandal followed the Vietnam War. Some historians claim that together the Vietnam War and Watergate dramatically reduced citizens' level of trust in their government, especially trust in their elected officials.

A. Do you believe the Vietnam War and Watergate diminished people's trust in their elected officials? Give evidence for your opinion.

B. Compare the public mood during the Vietnam and the Watergate years to the mood today. Do you think people today trust their elected officials more or less than they did then? In general, do you trust today's elected officials?

C. How could your trust in government, especially elected officials, be improved?

D. Is it both healthy and necessary for citizens to maintain some degree of distrust in their government? How much distrust is appropriate?

E. What recent events have either supported or eroded trust in government?

About the Activity

In this activity, students examine specific trends and analyze the implications of the trends for future social planning.

After participating in the activity, students will be able to:

■ identify some current trends and issues in the United States.

■ recognize implications of the trends for the nation's future.

■ describe how trend projection can be used in social planning.

Planning for the Activity

Suggested Time: 3 to 4 class periods

Materials: Activity Sheets 31a through 31c, one each per student

Advance Preparation: This activity requires students to review daily newspapers for about three weeks. Assign the newspaper review task about three weeks before you wish to complete the activity. An alternative strategy is suggested in the fourth teacher note.

THE ACTIVITY

Getting Started

Introduce the activity by asking students to list ways in which people try to predict the future. Record their responses on the chalkboard. Ask students to explain why people try to predict their own and society's future. Finally, ask students whether they think predicting the future is possible.

Teaching

Explain to the class that in this activity they will be looking at the future in the way people called *futurists* look ahead in time. Emphasize that futurists are not mystics but instead scientists with a special interest in the future. Futurists do not try to predict the future because they do not think prediction is possible. Rather, on the basis of available information gathered through sophisticated projection tools, they suggest possible futures that others can use for planning purposes.

Tell students that in this activity they will use a simple trend projection. They will identify and follow a trend, forecast its future, and suggest ways of dealing with the trend.

1. Distribute copies of Activity Sheet 31a. Tell students that the forecasts are a few of many made by futurists in the 1968 book *Toward the Year 2000*. See Additional Background Information for more detail.

COMMENTS/NOTES

Methods of prediction students suggest may include palm reading, crystal balls, tarot cards, tea leaf reading, horoscopes, and psychic predictions.

Background. The Commission of the Year 2000 was a committee formed by the American Academy of Arts and Sciences in the mid 1960s to look at the future of our country. The commission conducted a series of working

Have students follow the directions on the sheet. After they have assessed the forecasts, lead a class discussion. Challenge them to provide examples to support their own assessments of which 1968 forecasts have been realized.

2. Ask students to review their texts to identify trends and issues from the 1980s to the present. List these on the chalkboard. Challenge students to suggest others, and add those to the list.

3. Divide students into groups of about four students each. Assign, or allow groups to choose, a trend identified on the chalkboard. Provide each student with a copy of Activity Sheet 31b. Explain that during the next three weeks students are to track their assigned or chosen trends by reviewing newspapers daily for articles or commentaries related to them. They are to record relevant information on the chart on the activity sheet.

Point out that by identifying the amount of space (column inches) they can get a sense of the amount of attention being given the trend in the press. Direct students to continue their charts on additional sheets of notebook paper after they have used all the space on the activity sheet.

4. When the tracking period is over, reconvene the groups for the purpose of compiling individual students' information. Distribute copies of Activity Sheet 31c. Instruct students to discuss the questions in their groups, sharing information they collected in their trend tracking. After their small group discussion, require students to individually complete the activity sheet questions.

5. When students are finished with the activity sheet questions, ask spokespersons from the groups to share with the class information about the trends they studied. Encourage students to ask questions about and respond to the information presented.

6. To summarize, ask the following questions:

- Of what value are attempts to forecast the future?
- Based on the class's trend tracking, how would you characterize the future?
- What changes or factors in society seem to be most responsible for current trends?
- How can the public's interest in trends and future planning be increased?

Concluding

Write the following statement on the chalkboard:

The past cannot be influenced; it is finished. The present is happening, and it's too late to make significant changes in it. The future is the only period of time over which we have any control.

sessions to study trends and make forecasts for life in the United States in the year 2000. The forecasts on Activity Sheet 31a come from this committee's work.

Trends or issues students might identify include political conservatism, supply side economics, deregulation, decrease in federal spending, judicial conservatism, decline in the threat of communism, increase in drug use, spread of AIDS, growing numbers of homeless, recession, increased costs of higher education, growing elderly population, and soaring health care costs.

To reduce the length of time in which students track trends, have students begin to bring daily newspapers to class about three weeks before the activity is introduced. Students can then review the collected newspapers in one or two class periods.

Instruct students to respond in a one-paragraph statement. Tell them that in their paragraph they should agree or disagree with the statement, explain their position, and describe the implication of their position for the way we behave as individuals and as a society.

Evaluating Student Work

Students' participation may be assessed on both their group and individual work.

- Evaluation criteria for group work should include evidence of daily trend tracking and cooperativeness in working with other group members to summarize and analyze tracking information.

- Evaluation criteria for response paragraphs should include clarity of the position taken and logic in citing implications of the position.

Additional Background Information

In the book *Toward the Year 2000: Work in Progress,* edited by Daniel Bell and published in 1968, a committee of futurists compiled scientific, technological, and social forecasts. In summarizing their forecasts, the committee identified the following four major changes or sources of change they felt would significantly affect the future of the United States:

- the advancement of technology and related technological revolution
- the realization of the promise of equality
- centralization of the American political system
- increased interaction between the United States and other nations

155

On the Trail of a Trend
Reviewing Forecasts from 1968

Directions:

The statements below are forecasts that were made by a group of futurists in a 1968 book entitled *Toward the Year 2000*. The futurists predicted that their forecasts would be realized by the year 2000.

Review the list of forecasts and assess whether each has already been realized, is likely to be realized by the year 2000, or seems unlikely to ever be realized. Indicate your assessment of each forecast by writing its number beside the appropriate category below.

1968 Forecasts for the Year 2000

1. New techniques for preserving or improving the environment will be in use.

2. Humans will hibernate for short periods (hours or days) for medical purposes.

3. Nuclear reactors will be widely used to provide power for homes and industry.

4. Japan will emerge as a dominant world force.

5. The positions of the United States and the Soviet Union as world powers will decline.

6. The possibility of sustained mass movements will be greater. Such movements may revolve around idealist, messianic leaders or social policies such as nativism, the policy of favoring native inhabitants over immigrants.

7. People will increase their interest in the "meaning and purpose" of their personal and societal actions.

8. Home computers will "run" households and serve as communication links between families and the outside world.

9. Satellites will broadcast programming directly to home receivers.

10. Advanced defense systems will operate from space rather than land bases.

Forecasts already realized: _____

Forecasts likely to be realized by the year 2000: _____

Forecasts not likely to ever be realized: _____

On the Trail of a Trend
Tracking Trends

Directions:

Track your assigned trend each day by reviewing newspapers to find articles and commentaries on the subject. When you identify relevant information, record it in the chart below. Continue your chart on additional paper as required.

Date	News Source	Length of Article (column inches)	Summary

On the Trail of a Trend
Using Trends in Future Planning

Directions:

In small groups review the trend information you collected on Activity Sheet 31b. Use the information to answer the following questions:

1. Which group or groups of Americans are now, or will be in the future, most affected by the trend? How are they being affected?

_____

_____

_____

_____

2. What are potential social and financial benefits of the trend?

_____

_____

_____

_____

3. What are potential social and financial costs of the trend?

_____

_____

_____

_____

4. Should the trend be discouraged or should it be promoted?

_____

_____

_____

_____

5. Does the trend need to be managed? If so, what steps should be taken? Who should manage the trend?

_____

_____

_____

_____

Every Picture Tells a Story
Reviewing American History in a Collage

About the Activity

What is the big picture of American history? Working in small groups, students create thematic collages to summarize what they have learned in this course.

After participating in the activity, students will be able to

- identify unifying themes of American history.
- exemplify the themes with specific events or topics.

Planning for the Activity

Suggested Time: 2 class periods

Materials: large poster paper sheets taped together; color markers and pencils

THE ACTIVITY

Getting Started

Near the end of the term, form small groups of three to five students. Explain that to review the entire course they will work as a group to design and create a collage that summarizes what they have learned.

Teaching

Explain to students that their collages are to focus on a central unifying theme of American history. Discuss the nature of unifying themes as "big ideas." As examples, suggest the themes of balancing unity and diversity, shaping democracy, and searching for economic opportunity for all Americans. Suggest that students carefully review their text to identify unifying themes and to look for events and topics that illustrate those themes.

1. Outline the following steps groups are to follow in creating their collages.

Step 1 Select a unifying or overall theme for your collage. Decide how to illustrate the theme.

Step 2 Identify events and topics that indicate your collage's unifying theme. Decide how to illustrate those events or topics to enhance your collage. Because you cannot represent everything you have learned in one collage, you must be selective.

Step 3 On notebook paper, create a rough sketch of your proposed collage.

Step 4 Submit your preliminary sketch for teacher approval. Do not proceed with your actual collage before you have approval.

NOTES

Step 5 Upon receiving approval, collect your group's collage supplies and begin work on your final collage.

2. Share with students the criteria on which their collages will be evaluated. Some possible criteria are:

- The collage must have a title that conveys the theme.
- The collage may include original student illustrations, photocopies of pictures from books, and pictures from magazines and newspapers.
- Although artistic ability will not count, neatness and completeness of the presentation will count.
- The final product must reflect the work of all group members.

3. Set due dates for preliminary sketches and for final collages.

Concluding

Allow each group a minute or two to explain their collages to the class. After the presentations, point out how the collages provide a review of much of the course.

Evaluating Student Work

Although the evaluation of the collages does not need to be rigorous, assessments should be based on the criteria suggested in the Teaching section.

46632142R00095